The Architecture of Coherence

Emergence, Consciousness, and the Hidden Order Shaping Reality

VOLUME II

How Wholeness Arises—and Why It Changes Everything

SHREE SHAMBAV

The Architecture of Coherence
Emergence, Consciousness, and the Hidden Order Shaping Reality
Volume Two

Shree Shambav

Published by Shree Shambav, Tamil Nadu, India
Shree Shambav Ink & Imagination "Where Words Breathe and Imagination Soars"

First Edition, 2026

ISBN: 978-93-5780-880-4
Email:shreeshambav@gmail.com
Web:www.shambav.org

DEDICATION

"Isavasyam idam sarvam yat kim ca jagatyam jagat, tena tyaktena bhunjitha, ma gridhah kasyasvid dhanam"

To the Almighty,

the Divine Masters,

the family who listens,

and my parents who see –

your presence shapes the pages of my life's journey.

"Isavasyam idam sarvam yat kim ca jagatyam jagat"

Meaning: "God encompasses everything you perceive, see, or touch with your sense organs."

DISCLAIMER

The Architecture of Coherence is a philosophical and interdisciplinary exploration of emergence, coherence, and the formation of meaningful wholes across nature, mind, society, and technology. It arises from the author's integrative inquiry into philosophy, science, systems theory, and reflective understanding of reality. This work is offered as an invitation to contemplation and inquiry, not as a declaration of absolute or final truth.

The content of this book is intended solely for intellectual reflection, philosophical exploration, and educational enrichment. While it engages with concepts from physics, biology, neuroscience, and social systems, it does not present itself as a scientific textbook, empirical proof, or professional authority. Nothing within these pages should be interpreted as medical, psychological, legal, financial, technical, or therapeutic advice, nor as a substitute for consultation with qualified professionals.

Although care has been taken to present ideas with clarity, rigour, and good faith, the author makes no guarantees regarding the accuracy, completeness, or universal applicability of the interpretations offered. The frameworks and perspectives presented are exploratory and integrative by nature, and readers are encouraged to evaluate them critically and independently. Any conclusions, interpretations, or applications drawn from this work remain the sole responsibility of the reader.

Discussions of consciousness, emergence, social systems, ethics, and civilizational futures may invite deep reflection or challenge existing assumptions. Such responses are a natural part of philosophical engagement and are intended to foster awareness and understanding, not certainty or distress. Readers are encouraged to approach the material with discernment, openness, and intellectual humility.

This book does not seek to persuade, convert, or impose belief. It does not claim authority over scientific, philosophical, or spiritual truth. Rather, it offers a conceptual lens—a structured way of seeing—through which readers may explore the dynamics of coherence and collapse in both inner and outer worlds.

Ultimately, *The Architecture of Coherence* is shared in a spirit of inquiry and respect, trusting the reader's wisdom to integrate what resonates, question what does not, and engage with the material as a living dialogue rather than a fixed conclusion.

Note: For knowledge and contemplative purposes only.

Note - If any part of the book, in any sequence, hurts the reader's sentiments, it would be just out of a sheer accident not intentional

EPIGRAPH

The world does not ask to be controlled;

it asks to be understood in relation.

Where parts listen to wholes,

and wholes remain gentle with parts,

coherence breathes.

Meaning is not imposed from above—

it emerges when attention learns to stay.

– Shree Shambav

The Architecture of Coherence

Emergence, Consciousness, and the Hidden Order Shaping Reality

How Wholeness Arises—and Why It Changes Everything

SHREE SHAMBAV

Shree Shambav is a 130x best-selling author, renowned for his transformative works in personal development and spiritual growth

Dear Cherished Readers

Dear Cherished Readers,

As I embark on this new literary voyage, my heart swells with profound gratitude and an overwhelming sense of connection. With deep emotion, I extend my heartfelt appreciation to each of you who has joined me on this journey.

With sincere warmth, I invite you to revisit the steps we have taken together through the pages of my earlier works. Our odyssey began with "Journey of Soul - Karma," a book that marked my first foray into the world of words and a testament to the raw passion that ignited my writing adventure.

The subsequent chapters of our shared journey unfolded through the enchanting tapestry of the *"Twenty + One"* series. With each page turned, it felt as though a brushstroke was added to the canvas of our collective imagination—stories and sentiments woven to echo within the quiet corners of your heart. These weren't just words; they were invitations to feel, to reflect, and to remember what truly matters.

And how can I not cherish the transformative path we walked together through the *"Life Changing Journey—Inspirational Quotes Series?"* Day by day, quote by quote, we ventured inward—into spaces often overlooked—to find wisdom in simplicity and light in life's shadows. Each reflection was offered as a gentle whisper of hope, a spark meant to uplift, inspire, and remind us that even in silence, the soul speaks.

The release of "Death - Light of Life and the Shadow of Death" promises to shed new light on the timeless mystery of death.

The **Optimum Python Series** is a comprehensive learning pathway designed to empower readers at every stage of their programming journey. It begins with **Series I: Ultimate Guide for Beginners**, which builds a strong and accessible foundation in Python for newcomers. **Series II: Exploring Data Structures and Algorithms** advances into core computer science concepts, strengthening problem-solving skills and coding efficiency.

Building on this, **Series III: Python Power for Data Science** introduces powerful libraries such as NumPy, Pandas, Matplotlib, and Scikit-learn, guiding readers through data manipulation, visualisation, and foundational machine learning techniques. **Series IV:**

Unleashing the Potential of Data Science with Machine Learning Techniques explores advanced models and real-world applications.

This progression continues with **Series V: Optimum: Python Power – Unleashing the Potential of Data Science with Deep Learning Techniques**, and culminates in **Series VI: From Data to Intelligence – The Deep Learning Revolution**, enabling readers to harness the full potential of data-driven innovation. Whether you are a beginner or an advanced learner, this series serves as your complete roadmap to Python mastery and beyond.

Shree Shambav expands his artistic repertoire with *Whispers of Eternity: A Symphony of Soulful Verses*, a heartfelt exploration of the human experience expressed through lyrical depth and timeless reflection. Complementing this, his *Whispers of the Soul: A Journey Through Haiku* distils profound truths into delicate, poignant verses, capturing the fleeting essence of life with elegant simplicity.

Equally evocative, *Whispers of Stillness: Where the Soul Listens Beyond the Noise* offers meditative couplets that invite readers into silence, where wisdom blossoms in the spaces between words. Together, these works illuminate Shambav's versatility and mastery of soulful expression. They invite readers on a transformative journey of self-discovery, weaving a tapestry of emotion, insight, and transcendence that lingers long after the final page is turned.

Building on this success, he continued to enchant audiences with his subsequent albums: HeartStrings, *Melodies of the Heart*, *Driftwood Memories*, *Winds of Change, The Veil and the Waves, Echoes of the Soul, Phoenix Within,* Uncaged, Where Nature Sings, and Wings of Forever. Each album further solidified his place in the world of music, offering a mesmerising collection of tracks that evoke nostalgia, introspection, and heartfelt connection. With every composition, Shree Shambav weaves a musical journey that lingers in the soul long after the final note fades.

Shree Shambav's latest works shine as luminous beacons on the path of self-discovery, mindful living, and spiritual awakening. His writings span a vast spectrum of human experience, each book offering a doorway to transformation. Among his most celebrated titles are Learn to Love Yourself: A Journey of Discovering Inner Beauty and Strength Through 10 Transformative Rules, The Power of Letting Go: Embrace Freedom and Happiness, A Journey of Lasting Peace, and The Entitlement Trap: Get Over It, Get On.

His thought-provoking works include Whispers of a Dying Soul: Unspoken Regrets and Unlived Dreams, Whispers of Silence: Unlocking Inner Power through Stillness, The Power of Words: Transforming Speech,

Transforming Lives, The Art of Intentional Living: Minimalism for a Life of Purpose, and Awakening the Infinite: The Power of Consciousness in Transforming Life.

In The Power of Manifestation: Unlocking the Path from Thought to Reality, Shree Shambav presents a transformative roadmap for turning vision into lived experience, guiding readers from intention to realisation. Beyond the Veil: A Journey Through Life After Death ventures into the profound mystery of existence beyond the physical realm, inviting contemplation on life, transition, and the eternal soul.

His other compelling works include Bonds Beyond Blood: Where Love Builds Bridges and Bonds Defy Lineage, a heartfelt celebration of love that transcends ancestry and form; The Inner Battlefield: Overcoming the Enemies of the Mind and Soul, a powerful guide to mastering inner conflicts and reclaiming mental sovereignty; and A Journey into Spiritual Maturity: 12 Golden Rules for Inner Transformation, which offers timeless wisdom for seekers evolving toward self-mastery and inner awakening.

In The Seeker's Gold: Unlocking Life's Greatest Treasure, he inspires readers to uncover the hidden riches of the soul, while The Law of Attraction: A Soulful Path reveals how to harmonise thought, energy, and intention to create a life aligned with one's highest purpose. His transformative Born to Rise series further empowers readers to embrace growth, clarity, and lasting fulfilment across every dimension of life.

Shree Shambav is also the author of Mastering the Art of Gratitude: A Journey from Acknowledgment to Awakening, a contemplative series on conscious appreciation, and Whispers of a Silent Monk: Poetic Tales of Love, Loss, and Liberation, a lyrical exploration of silence, surrender, and inner freedom.

In addition, his works Journey of the Soul – Karma Unveiled, Unveiling the Enigma, and Death: Light of Life and the Shadow of Death have been translated into Gujarati and Hindi, extending his spiritual insights to a wider audience.

In addition to these works, Shree Shambav has recently ventured into astrology with the release of Astrology Unveiled – Foundations of Ancient Wisdom Series I to XIX, expanding into the realm of metaphysics. These books explore the foundational principles of Vedic astrology, offering readers a rich and practical understanding of this ancient wisdom.

Your unwavering support, enthusiasm to immerse yourself in my writings, and readiness to embark on these journeys with me have been my greatest sources of inspiration. Your input has been a beacon guiding me through the creation process, moulding these stories into containers of passion, emotion, knowledge, and resonance.

As I unveil this new narrative before you, know that your presence, insights, and shared moments have been my companions. The path we have walked together is etched in the annals of my creative evolution, and it's an honour beyond words to have you by my side once more.

Here's to the readers who have illuminated my path with their presence, who have embraced my stories with open hearts, and who have woven themselves into the very fabric of my literary world. Our journey has been a symbiotic dance of writer and reader, a harmony of souls brought together by the magic of storytelling.

With a heart brimming with appreciation and eyes glistening with anticipation, I extend my deepest gratitude for your unwavering support. Thank you for the memories, the shared emotions, and the countless hours spent in the worlds we've crafted together. As we step into this new adventure, let's continue to explore, feel, and discover the boundless horizons that words can unveil.

Warmly,

Shree Shambav

Suggested Reads

ENDORSEMENTS

A rare work that meets complexity without fear or false certainty.

The Architecture of Coherence offers a rigorous yet humane framework for understanding emergence across science, society, ethics, and consciousness. It neither reduces meaning to mechanics nor escapes into abstraction. Instead, it invites responsibility, humility, and care in how we think and act within interconnected systems. This book is not only timely—it is necessary for an age shaped by fragile coherence and accelerating change.

— Akshaya (IT)

About the Author

Shree Shambav is an internationally acclaimed best-selling author, inspirational speaker, artist, philanthropist, life coach, strategist, and entrepreneur. A world record holder, his deep passion for music led him to create soul-stirring albums, drawing inspiration from his celebrated poetry collection, Whispers of Eternity. His profound insights have sparked deep personal transformations, guiding countless individuals toward self-discovery, purposeful living, and authenticity.

With an extraordinary ability to unlock human potential, Shree empowers individuals to break through limitations and embrace their highest selves. His writings, lectures, and compassionate guidance continue to uplift lives, fostering resilience, mindfulness, and personal growth.

Shree Shambav is a 130x best-selling author celebrated for his profound contributions to personal development and spiritual growth.

Shree Shambav's literary journey took flight with the celebrated Journey of Soul - Karma, where he delved into the depths of human experience to unveil profound insights. Garnering recognition through multiple literature awards, his repertoire includes esteemed works, such as the Twenty + One Series, and the enlightening Life Changing Journey – Inspirational Quotes series.

As a distinguished alumnus of the Indian Institute of Management and the National Institute of Technology, Shree Shambav brings a wealth of corporate acumen from his tenure in multinational corporations. His most recent publications, including Unveiling the Enigma, Death - Light of Life and the Shadow of Death, and Optimum – Power Python Series I, Series II, Series III, Series IV, Series V, and Series VI, demonstrate his mastery of both the literary and technical spheres.

Shree Shambav expands his artistic repertoire with *Whispers of Eternity: A Symphony of Soulful Verses*, a heartfelt exploration of the human experience expressed through lyrical depth and timeless reflection. Complementing this, his *Whispers of the Soul: A Journey Through Haiku* distils profound truths into delicate, poignant verses, capturing the fleeting essence of life with elegant simplicity.

Equally evocative, *Whispers of Stillness: Where the Soul Listens Beyond the Noise* offers meditative couplets that invite readers into silence, where wisdom blossoms in the spaces between words. Together, these works illuminate Shambav's versatility and mastery of soulful expression. They invite readers on a transformative journey of self-discovery, weaving a tapestry of emotion, insight, and transcendence that lingers long after the final page is turned.

Building on this success, he continued to enchant audiences with his subsequent albums: HeartStrings, *Melodies of the Heart*, *Driftwood Memories*, *Winds of Change, The Veil and the Waves, Echoes of the Soul, Phoenix Within,* Uncaged, Where Nature Sings, and Wings of Forever. Each album further solidified his place in the world of music, offering a mesmerising collection of tracks that evoke nostalgia, introspection, and heartfelt connection. With every composition, Shree Shambav weaves a musical journey that lingers in the soul long after the final note fades.

Shree Shambav's latest works shine as luminous beacons on the path of self-discovery, mindful living, and spiritual awakening. His writings span a vast spectrum of human experience, each book offering a doorway to transformation. Among his most celebrated titles are Learn to Love Yourself: A Journey of Discovering Inner Beauty and Strength Through 10 Transformative Rules, The Power of Letting Go: Embrace Freedom and Happiness, A Journey of Lasting Peace, and The Entitlement Trap: Get Over It, Get On.

His thought-provoking works include Whispers of a Dying Soul: Unspoken Regrets and Unlived Dreams, Whispers of Silence: Unlocking Inner Power through Stillness, The Power of Words: Transforming Speech, Transforming Lives, The Art of Intentional Living: Minimalism for a Life of Purpose, and Awakening the Infinite: The Power of Consciousness in Transforming Life.

In The Power of Manifestation: Unlocking the Path from Thought to Reality, Shree Shambav presents a transformative roadmap for turning vision into lived experience, guiding readers from intention to realisation. Beyond the Veil: A Journey Through Life After Death ventures into the profound mystery of existence beyond the physical realm, inviting contemplation on life, transition, and the eternal soul.

His other compelling works include Bonds Beyond Blood: Where Love Builds Bridges and Bonds Defy Lineage, a heartfelt celebration of love that transcends ancestry and form; The Inner Battlefield: Overcoming the Enemies of the Mind and Soul, a powerful guide to mastering inner conflicts and reclaiming mental sovereignty; and A Journey into Spiritual Maturity: 12 Golden Rules for Inner Transformation, which offers timeless wisdom for seekers evolving toward self-mastery and inner awakening.

In The Seeker's Gold: Unlocking Life's Greatest Treasure, he inspires readers to uncover the hidden riches of the soul, while The Law of Attraction: A Soulful Path reveals how to harmonise thought, energy, and intention to create a life aligned with one's highest purpose. His transformative Born to Rise series further empowers readers to embrace growth, clarity, and lasting fulfilment across every dimension of life.

Shree Shambav is also the author of Mastering the Art of Gratitude: A Journey from Acknowledgment to Awakening, a contemplative series on conscious appreciation, and Whispers of a Silent Monk: Poetic Tales of Love, Loss, and Liberation, a lyrical exploration of silence, surrender, and inner freedom.

In addition, his works Journey of the Soul – Karma Unveiled, Unveiling the Enigma, and Death: Light of Life and the Shadow of Death have been translated into Gujarati and Hindi, extending his spiritual insights to a wider audience.

In addition to these works, Shree Shambav has recently ventured into astrology with the release of Astrology Unveiled – Foundations of Ancient Wisdom Series I to XVII, expanding into the realm of metaphysics. These books explore the foundational principles of Vedic astrology, offering readers a rich and practical understanding of this ancient wisdom.

Shree Shambav established the Ayur Rakshita Foundation, which is dedicated to promoting boundless growth, universal fraternity, and environmental protection. The charity helps diverse communities while working for societal progress.

To learn more about Shree Shambav and his works, visit his website at www.shambav.org. For information about the Ayur Rakshita Foundation and its initiatives, visit www.shambav-ayurrakshita.org.

Let's Follow him on Social Media: **@shreeshambav**

PREFACE

This book was not written to offer certainty. It was written to remain faithful to a tension.

Across disciplines—physics, biology, neuroscience, sociology, ethics—we have learned how to explain more and understand less. Knowledge has expanded horizontally while meaning has thinned vertically. We know *how* systems behave, yet struggle to say *what it means* that they do. This work arises from that fracture—not as an attempt to close it prematurely, but to stand within it honestly.

The Architecture of Coherence is born from a simple but unsettling observation: reality does not behave like a collection of independent parts. It behaves like a layered, interdependent unfolding in which patterns acquire causal power, meanings arise without designers, and wholes shape the very elements from which they emerge. Emergence is no longer a marginal idea. It sits quietly beneath our most urgent questions—about consciousness, society, technology, ethics, and the future itself.

Yet emergence alone is insufficient. Without coherence, it dissolves into relativism. Without constraint, it becomes noise. The central concern of this book is not merely that new properties arise, but that they *hold together*—sometimes beautifully, sometimes destructively. Coherence is what allows complexity to persist, but it is also what makes failure catastrophic when systems grow too tightly coupled.

This volume, in particular, turns its attention to pressure points. It asks what happens when emergent systems scale beyond the environments that shaped them, when institutions outlive their adaptability, when technologies outrun ethical reflection, and when responsibility becomes distributed so widely that it appears to vanish. These are not abstract concerns. They are the lived conditions of our time.

The chapters that follow do not offer blueprints. They resist the temptation to design the future from first principles. Instead, they explore patterns—how intelligence becomes collective, how fragility forms, how collapse shadows order, and how care might replace control as a governing ethic. The aim is not prediction, but orientation.

This book is written for readers who sense that reductionism no longer suffices, yet are wary of mysticism disguised as depth. It is for those who seek integration without dogma, humility without nihilism, and meaning without illusion. Scientific rigour and philosophical reflection are treated here not as rivals, but as complementary lenses through which coherence becomes visible.

If there is a quiet argument running beneath these pages, it is this: truth, when understood as coherence across scales, carries ethical weight. To see reality clearly is already to be implicated in it. Understanding cannot remain neutral when systems are interconnected, and consequences cascade beyond intention.

The reader is not positioned here as an observer standing outside the architecture being described. You are already inside it. Your thoughts, values, technologies, and institutions participate in the same emergent dynamics this book seeks to illuminate. To read about coherence is, inevitably, to be invited into responsibility.

This preface does not ask for agreement. It asks for patience. Coherence reveals itself slowly, often at the edges of discomfort, where certainty gives way to relationship. If this book succeeds, it will not convince you of a theory—it will alter the way you notice patterns, carry questions, and inhabit the systems you help sustain.

That, ultimately, is the only preface coherence requires.

With kindest regards,

Shree Shambav

CONTENTS

INTRODUCTION

In earlier explorations of emergence, coherence often appears as a promise—an elegant principle capable of explaining how complexity arises from simplicity, how minds emerge from matter, how meaning grows from interaction. Yet coherence is not merely something that appears when conditions are favourable. It is something that must endure strain. And it is under pressure that its true nature is revealed.

Volume II: Coherence Under Pressure turns toward those moments when emergent systems are stressed, distorted, or pushed beyond the environments that once sustained them. Societies polarise, institutions ossify, technologies amplify unintended consequences, and ethical responsibility diffuses across networks so vast that no single agent seems accountable. These are not failures at the margins of emergence; they are its central trials.

The chapters that follow explore a sobering truth: systems rarely collapse into chaos. More often, they fail by becoming *too* coherent in the wrong way. Patterns harden. Feedback loops narrow. Adaptability gives way to rigidity. What once coordinated intelligence begins to amplify error. Fragility, in this sense, is not the absence of order but the persistence of maladaptive order.

This volume examines society not as a designed artifact but as a living, emergent organism—one that grows through decentralised interactions, shared meanings, and invisible norms. It asks why such systems sometimes achieve collective wisdom and, at other times, descend into collective delusion. It confronts the paradox of hierarchy: why top-down control repeatedly reasserts itself in systems that arise bottom-up, not as a betrayal of emergence, but as a structural pressure inherent to large-scale coordination.

The inquiry then moves to failure itself—not as an anomaly, but as the shadow of organisation. From biological systems to institutions and technologies, collapse is revealed as a predictable companion to coherence, shaped by thresholds, mismatches, and cascading interactions. Resilience, when it appears, is shown not as resistance to change, but as the capacity to reorganise meaningfully under stress.

As human beings increasingly attempt to *design* emergent systems—artificial intelligence, digital economies, global platforms—the limits of control become unavoidable. Optimisation produces second-order consequences. Alignment proves dynamic rather than fixed. The deeper lesson emerges quietly but insistently: emergence cannot be engineered, only cultivated.

The final movement of this volume widens the lens to ethics and futures. When harm, agency, and responsibility arise from systems rather than individuals, moral thought must evolve. Ethics becomes less about judging actions and more about stewarding conditions. Flourishing is redefined as nested coherence—the sustained alignment of systems across scales, from minds to societies to ecosystems.

Ultimately, this volume leads toward a synthesis: *coherent emergentism* not as a theory to admire, but as an orientation to live by. If coherence truly shapes reality, then truth cannot remain abstract. It must be expressed in governance, technology, education, and daily conduct. The question this book leaves the reader with is not whether emergence explains the world—but whether we are willing to become coherent participants within it.

This is not a book about control. It is a book about humility before complexity, responsibility within interdependence, and the fragile, luminous patterns that hold reality together—until they are asked to hold more than they can bear.

Warm regards,

Shree Shambav

PROLOGUE

When the Whole Appears

Before there were theories, there were patterns.

Before equations, there were rhythms—day and night, breath and heartbeat, growth and decay. Long before human language learned to name the world, the world was already arranging itself into forms that endured. Nothing instructed rivers how to carve valleys. Nothing designed the murmuration of birds or the spiral of a galaxy. And yet, order appeared—not imposed, but arising.

We have spent centuries trying to understand reality by breaking it apart. This approach has given us extraordinary power. It has taught us how matter behaves, how life evolves, how neurons fire, and how markets move. But it has also trained us to overlook something essential: the way parts become wholes, and how those wholes begin to matter.

A thought is not found in a neuron. A society is not contained in a person. Meaning does not reside in a molecule. These are not failures of measurement; they are features of emergence. The world is layered, and each layer carries properties that cannot be reduced without being erased.

Yet emergence is not chaos. Patterns do not merely appear; they stabilise, interact, and constrain what comes next. Coherence is the quiet force that allows complexity to persist—to remember itself across time. It is what keeps a body alive, a language intelligible, a culture recognisable. And it is also what allows systems to fail spectacularly when coherence hardens into rigidity or accelerates beyond its capacity to adapt.

We now live inside systems whose coherence exceeds our comprehension. Global economies, digital networks, artificial intelligences, and ecological feedback loops—none were designed as totalities, yet all exert real causal power over human lives. No single actor controls them. No single intention governs their outcomes. Responsibility has become distributed, and with it, uncertainty has deepened.

This book begins from that unsettled ground.

It does not ask whether emergence is real—that question has already been answered by the sciences. It asks what emergence *demands* of us when its consequences become ethical, political, and existential.

What does responsibility mean when harm arises without malice? How do we govern systems that cannot be fully predicted? What kind of intelligence is required to live within patterns we did not design but continuously reinforce?

The chapters that follow trace an invisible architecture one built not of steel or code, but of relationships, feedback, and constraint. They move across scales, from cells to civilisations, from neural dynamics to moral responsibility, from spiritual experience to technological futures. The aim is not to replace reduction with mysticism, nor certainty with relativism, but to articulate a framework capable of holding complexity without collapsing into either.

Coherent emergentism is not offered here as a doctrine, but as an orientation: a way of seeing reality as a nested unfolding in which meaning arises through relation, and truth reveals itself through alignment rather than domination. It is an invitation to notice not only what things are made of, but how they hold together—and at what cost.

There is no vantage point outside this inquiry. To understand emergence is to recognise oneself as an emergent process, shaped by systems that both enable and constrain choice. The reader is not separate from the architecture described here; you are one of its active nodes.

This prologue marks the threshold of that recognition.

What follows is not a map of certainty, but a discipline of attention—an effort to listen for coherence in a world strained by its own complexity, and to ask, with seriousness and care, how such coherence might yet be lived.

Warm regards,

Shree Shambav

Prelude

There are moments when the world feels as though it is coming apart—not in noise or explosion, but in subtle misalignment. Institutions still stand, technologies still function, language still circulates, yet something essential feels strained, brittle, overextended. We sense it in fractured discourse, in systems that optimise relentlessly yet fail humanly, in progress that accelerates even as meaning thins. These moments do not announce collapse; they whisper incoherence.

This book was born in such a moment.

Not from a single crisis, but from a convergence: knowledge advancing faster than wisdom, connectivity deepening alongside alienation, power scaling beyond accountability. We understand more than ever, yet we struggle to integrate what we know. The problem is no longer ignorance. It is fragmentation.

Science explains the world with extraordinary precision, yet often brackets meaning. Philosophy interrogates meaning, yet can drift from empirical grounding. Ethics seeks responsibility, yet is overwhelmed by systems no individual controls.

Spiritual traditions speak of wholeness, yet risk disengagement from material reality. Each discipline sharpens its own lens, and the sky fractures into pieces no one can fully reassemble.

The intuition guiding this work is simple but demanding: reality does not fragment itself—*we* do, by the way we carve it for understanding. Beneath our divisions, the world continues to organise, relate, and respond as a whole. Emergence is the name we give to this quiet persistence of pattern—how coherence arises without command, how meaning appears without design, how order survives within flux.

Yet emergence is not inherently benevolent. The same processes that generate life, intelligence, and cooperation can also amplify rigidity, inequality, and systemic harm. Coherence, when unexamined, can become a trap. This is the tension at the heart of our time: systems grow more interconnected even as our capacity to guide them lags behind.

This prelude is not an argument, but a pause—a moment of orientation before descent. It asks the reader to suspend the expectation of final answers and instead cultivate a different posture: one attentive to relationships rather than objects, to conditions rather than endpoints, to patterns rather than parts.

The pages ahead will move across scales and domains, but their concern is singular: how coherence forms, how it fails, and how it might be lived responsibly under pressure. The inquiry is rigorous, but its stakes are human. It is about how we design technologies, how we govern societies, how we interpret consciousness, and how we situate ourselves within a world that no longer tolerates simplistic control.

To read this book is not merely to acquire a framework. It is to enter a conversation with complexity itself—to notice where coherence already exists, where it has turned brittle, and where it might yet be cultivated through care, humility, and ethical attention.

Before theory, there is listening.

Before control, there is participation.

Before mastery, there is coherence.

This is the ground from which the journey begins.

At Kanchipuram

"No single step turns a walk into a journey. Yet somewhere along the way, motion becomes direction."

- Shree Shambav.

The morning in Kanchipuram did not arrive abruptly. It revealed itself slowly, reverently, as though time itself were reluctant to disturb the sanctity of what was unfolding.

During **Brahma Muhurtam**—that sacred hinge between night and day—the land rested in a hush so complete it felt intentional. Darkness still lingered, but it had softened, thinning into a deep velvety blue. Night was no longer resisting dawn; it was bowing to it. Mist hovered close to the earth, veiling dew-drenched grass that shimmered faintly, each blade holding a silent offering. The air was cool, almost tender, carrying the quiet fragrance of damp soil and unseen blossoms. A gentle breeze moved through the branches, setting them into a slow, contemplative dance, as if the trees themselves were stretching awake.

Beneath the ancient banyan tree, **Akshaya** and **Kiran** sat cross-legged on the cool, receptive ground. The banyan's aerial roots descended like the matted locks of an ascetic lost in timeless meditation. It was more than a tree—it was a witness. Older than memory, patient beyond lifetimes, it carried within its silence the residue of countless seekers who had passed through this land, leaving behind nothing but breath, intention, and the faint echo of surrender.

The earth beneath them felt alive—not metaphorically, but tangibly—pulsing with a quiet awareness. Without instruction or signal, their eyes closed. Spines aligned. Breath slowed, settling into a rhythm older than language, older than thought. They were not *practising* meditation; meditation was unfolding through them. The banyan did not merely shade their bodies—it sheltered their remembering.

One by one, others arrived.

Vasudeva approached first, his footsteps measured, almost ceremonial, as though silence itself were a fragile vessel he wished to enter without fracture. **Vidyarthi** followed, carrying the unspoken ease of one who had already arrived inwardly long before reaching this place. No greetings were exchanged. No acknowledgements were necessary. At that hour, even names felt excessive. Presence alone was sufficient.

Time loosened its grip.

An hour passed—not marked by clocks, but by the dissolving of effort, by the thinning of thought, by the moment attention ceased searching and began resting. When eyes finally opened, there was no dramatic return. What appeared instead was a quiet luminosity—the stillness of inner waters that had settled completely. It was not happiness, not bliss, but something rarer and truer: the feeling of being at home within oneself.

Their morning walk followed—not as exercise, but as **prayer in motion**. Each step was deliberate, unhurried, as though the earth beneath their feet were sacred scripture and they were reading it line by line. No one spoke. Silence walked with them—not as absence, but as a companion.

As they neared the temple grounds, silence did not break.

It transformed.

Bhajans drifted through the air from **Shambav Bhajan**—the tabla and dholak laying down steady heartbeats, the harmonium breathing long devotional phrases. **Om** rose and fell from Zen meditation—not merely chanted but embodied—rippling through stone, air, and bone alike. Temple bells rang—round and generous—each peal dissolving into the next, as though time itself were being gently awakened.

The fragrance of flowers, sandalwood, and incense moved freely—curling around pillars, brushing skin, settling into breath. Holiness was not imposed here; it was ambient, like oxygen. One did not enter it. One realised they had always been within it.

Nearby, devotees moved through yogic postures, bodies rising and folding like verses written in muscle and breath. Others tended the gardens, hands deep in soil, leaves brushed aside with care. No task felt lesser. Stillness and action were simply two expressions of the same devotion.

Morning in Kanchipuram did not begin as an ordinary day.
It unfolded—slowly, reverently—like a forgotten hymn remembered by the soul before the mind could claim it.

A cool breeze flowed through the temple streets, carrying the scent of damp earth and last night's rain, softened by jasmine. Tiny streams murmured beside stone paths, telling stories that had never required listeners. Leaves held dewdrops like quiet offerings. Birds perched in readiness—not yet singing, but listening.

In the distance, **Aastha**, **Abhirami**, **Kiran**, **Sam**, and **Akshatha** wandered through Brindavan Garden. Flowers swayed as if responding to an unheard raga, petals bending beneath the weight of dew—reluctant to release the night, yet eager for the day.

From the temple steps emerged **Akshatha**, **Nita**, **Lalitha**, **Rohith**, and **Sujitha**, their bhajans still echoing softly within their chests. Soon after, **Roopa**, **Kieron**, **Astyn**, **Espen**, **Greta**, and **Divyani** arrived from their yoga practice—bodies warm, breath aligned, eyes clear—each carrying the quiet harmony that arises when breath and being agree. Moments later, **Aurora**, **Ginevra**, **Emma**, **Giorgia**, **Greta**, **Martina**, and **Beatrice** joined, their presence gentle, unforced, as if the morning itself had called them by name.

This was not a gathering.

It was a remembering.

The air itself seemed to whisper:

All that you have sought has always been here.

The sun did not rise. It arrived—like an honoured guest—offering warmth not as command but as blessing. The sky softened, melting into gold like ghee into flame. The earth exhaled, long and contented, as footsteps echoed gently—seekers arriving not at a place, but at a moment.

Sofia, **Bhavya**, and **Akanksh** walked the gravel path—not as wanderers, but as pilgrims responding to a call older than memory. Neem leaves rustled overhead, their sound forming a tanpura drone, tuning the morning itself. Even the banyans seemed to bow inwardly, roots heavy with remembrance, welcoming souls they had known across lifetimes.

Silence accompanied them—not emptiness, but fullness.
A silence that listened.

Then **Aurora** smiled—a small, effortless curve of warmth.

"Shall we begin with coffee?" she asked.

The words landed gently, like a bell rung not to awaken the world, but to invite it closer. Cups of steaming coffee and tea appeared, glowing like small lamps, warmth travelling from palms to hearts.

Birdsong finally rose—slow, devotional—the *alaap* of the morning raga. Sandalwood mingled with neem blossoms. Soft laughter flowed as **Aarna**, **Dev**, and **John** joined, their presence light and unburdened—sunlight translated into sound.

After a pause that felt complete, **Akanksh** spoke, his voice steady with reverence.

"Guruji will be continuing from the previous session—on *Emergence, Consciousness, and the Hidden Order Shaping Reality.*"

Nods moved through the circle—not agreement, but readiness.

A deeper hush followed.

Apeksha lifted her gaze toward the banyan canopy, where sunlight filtered through leaves like liquid gold. When her eyes returned to the circle, something subtle had shifted—as though an unseen door had opened quietly within the day itself.

Before she could speak, **Emma's** voice rose—low, tender, almost a vibration rather than sound.

"Apeksha," she said softly, "please… tell us a story to begin our day."

Apeksha did not begin immediately.

Silence gathered—full, attentive, alive.

Then she spoke.

"Once," she began, "there was a village that believed dawn arrived when the sun appeared. But the elders knew better. They said dawn comes earlier—when the world first remembers itself."

No one shifted. Even the birds seemed to pause.

She continued, her gaze moving slowly across the circle, not fixing on faces but touching something behind them.

"In that village lived a potter who woke each day before light. He did not wake because he was disciplined, nor because he feared missing the day. He woke because the clay beneath his hands had begun calling him in his sleep. The clay did not speak in words. It spoke in readiness."

A breeze moved through the banyan's roots, brushing their shoulders.

"The potter never asked what the clay would become. A bowl, a lamp, a vessel for water—those were decisions made later. First came listening. He would sit in silence, palms resting on the cool earth, until his breath and the clay's patience became one rhythm. Only then would form emerge."

Apeksha paused, letting the image settle.

"Consciousness," she said gently, "is like that clay. Not born when thought appears, not defined by what it becomes—but present when coherence gathers enough stillness to hold a shape."

Something shifted in the air—subtle, unmistakable.

She looked toward Akshaya and Kiran.

"The potter's wheel spun because of force," she continued, "but the vessel held because of balance. Too much pressure, and it collapsed. Too little, and it never rose. Freedom was not the absence of constraint—it was the harmony of forces agreeing for a moment."

Beatrice lowered her eyes, her breath deepening. Martina's hands rested loosely in her lap, as though holding an invisible warmth.

"This is how the mind works," Apeksha said. "Neurons fire, laws operate, causes unfold. Yet somewhere within that lawful movement, coherence appears—not as rebellion against causality, but as its flowering. Like the river shaped by its banks, awareness moves freely because it is held."

The temple bells rang again in the distance—softer now, as if responding rather than announcing.

"And the hard problem we fear," she added, her voice almost a whisper, "is often not a wall, but a mirror. We ask why experience exists, forgetting that the question itself is already experience asking after its own reflection."

Aurora's earlier question hovered unspoken in the space between them, now answered not with argument, but with recognition.

"When coherence becomes aware of itself," Apeksha said, "it does not shout. It simply knows. Like dawn knowing it has arrived—long before the sun agrees."

Silence returned, fuller than before. Not empty. Complete.

The banyan stood unmoving, roots descending deep into unseen soil, leaves lifting toward widening light—binding earth and sky without effort.

Aarna exhaled again, this time with a faint smile.

"It's time," he said softly.

No one hurried. No one resisted.

Guruji's morning session awaited—but something essential had already begun. Not in words, not in teachings, but in the quiet coherence now shared among them.

Kanchipuram breathed on—bells, birds, banyan, breath—each part distinct, yet inseparable from the whole.

And in that living rhythm, the day did not merely start.

It remembered itself.

Note: Hereafter, Shree Shambav will be referred to as 'Guruji' means Master.

PART ONE

EMERGENT SYSTEMS UNDER STRAIN

When coherence fractures—or mutates

"True listening is not the act of hearing words, but the quiet alignment where meaning reveals itself without being spoken."

- *Shree Shambav*

CHAPTER I

Social Wholes Without Designers

"A crowd can solve problems no individual can, or forget what no one intended to lose."

– Shree Shambav.

Synopsis

Societies are not engineered; they arise. This chapter explores how coherent social structures emerge from decentralised individual actions, forming an invisible architecture of norms, markets, and shared meanings. While such systems often display remarkable coordination, their intelligence is fragile. Under certain conditions, collectives amplify wisdom; under others, they magnify error.

The chapter examines why some groups achieve swarm intelligence while others descend into polarisation and collective irrationality. Attention then turns to institutions—legal systems, governments, and cultural frameworks—as emergent entities that exert real causal influence over individuals, despite existing only as abstractions.

Finally, the chapter confronts a persistent paradox: if societies emerge bottom-up, why do top-down hierarchies continually reassert themselves? Rather than dismissing emergence, this recurrence reveals structural pressures within social systems themselves. Society, the chapter concludes, behaves less like a machine and more like an organism—capable of coherence, adaptation, and systemic disease.

The devotees had settled into the Buddha Hall, not only in posture but in attention. Spines were upright, breaths natural and unforced, eyes resting in a soft openness that comes when effort falls away. The hall itself felt attentive, its high ceiling holding the silence steadily, without tension or distraction.

After a few quiet moments, Guruji entered.

There was no announcement. There never was.

His presence was felt before it was noticed. A gentle smile rested on his face, not directed toward anyone in particular, yet received by everyone. With folded palms, he offered Atma Namaskar—not as a formal greeting, but as recognition: awareness acknowledging itself through many forms.

He paused briefly at the centre of the hall. The pause gathered the room. Then, with ease and simplicity, he took his asana. A collective exhale moved through the hall, as though one body had relaxed.

Silence settled—stable, open, and alive.

When Guruji spoke, his voice was calm and unhurried. It carried no force, no demand for attention—only clarity.

Guruji said, "Before you try to understand society," Guruji began, his voice low and unhurried, "you must first let go of the idea that it was ever *designed*."

The hall was quiet. Not the silence of waiting, but the silence of listening.

"Imagine," he continued, "standing on a hill at dawn, overlooking a vast city. Roads twist like rivers. Lights flicker awake in windows. Vendors set out their goods. Trains arrive and depart. A million lives begin moving—each with purpose, urgency, fear, hope. Now ask yourself: *Who planned this?*"

He paused.

"No one," he said softly. "And yet—look at the order."

He gestured as if tracing invisible streets in the air.

"No single mind drew the whole city. No master blueprint predicted where every shop would stand, where lovers would meet, where protests would erupt, or where silence would survive. And yet the city breathes. It feeds itself. It repairs itself. It remembers."

Guruji's eyes moved slowly across the listeners.

"Society is like this city. It is not a machine assembled from above. It is an organism grown from below."

He leaned forward slightly.

"Every greeting exchanged, every fear passed down, every rule followed or broken—these are the cells of the social body. Individually, they seem insignificant. Together, they form arteries of power, habits of thought, cultures of belief. The order does not arrive through the command. It *condenses* through repetition."

A faint smile touched his face.

"Just as no single ant understands the colony, no single citizen understands society. And yet the colony builds. The society governs. Intelligence emerges where no intelligence was placed."

Then his tone shifted—gentler, but heavier.

"But understand this," he said, "emergent organisms can fall ill."

A ripple of attention moved through the room.

"When coherence hardens, it becomes rigidity. When coordination loses reflection, it becomes control. What once enabled life can begin to suffocate it."

He raised his hand slightly, palm open.

"Consider a city whose roads were once pathways of connection. Over time, traffic thickens. Movement slows. What was designed by no one now traps everyone. No villain is required. No conspiracy is necessary. Pathology emerges simply because the system continues obeying patterns that no longer serve it."

His voice softened.

"Societal suffering rarely comes from evil intent. It comes from *inherited coherence*—from structures that persist long after their wisdom has expired."

He looked toward the window, where light filtered in.

"Institutions, laws, markets, traditions—they begin as solutions. They become habits. Then they become identities. And finally, they become prisons that no one remembers building."

A long pause followed.

"Do not mistake emergence for innocence," Guruji said. "A system without a designer still has consequences. A body without awareness can still wound itself."

He turned back to the circle.

"This is why societies oscillate between freedom and hierarchy. Between openness and control. When coherence loosens, chaos threatens. When it tightens, life suffocates. The organism is always seeking balance—but it does so blindly."

His voice lowered, almost a whisper.

"And here is the hardest truth," he said. "No one is fully responsible. And everyone is involved."

He let that settle.

"To live ethically within society is not to dominate it, nor to escape it—but to listen for where coherence has turned brittle, where patterns persist without compassion."

He smiled again—this time with quiet warmth.

"Society does not need a new architect," Guruji said. "It needs new *sensitivities*."

The hall remained still.

Outside, the city continued—unaware of itself, yet alive; unplanned, yet patterned; capable of care, and capable of harm.

And somewhere within that vast, breathing organism, awareness had just grown a little deeper.

The hall was quiet in that particular way silence becomes when a question has already begun forming long before it is spoken. Lamps along the walls flickered gently, their flames steady, as though even fire had learned restraint in Guruji's presence. Outside, the evening wind brushed the neem leaves, creating a soft, restless murmur—like a city heard from far away.

Guruji had been speaking of society, not as a structure or system, but as something alive. Then Padma rose, palms folded, her voice carrying both curiosity and unease.

"Guruji," she asked, "how do individual actions—without centralised design—generate coherent social structures like markets, norms, or language? Is this spontaneous order truly emergent, or is it merely the aggregation of individual intentions?"

Guruji smiled, not immediately answering. He looked toward the far end of the hall, where the open doors framed the darkening sky. For a moment, it felt as though he was listening not to Padma's words, but to the question beneath them.

Then he spoke.

"Have you ever walked through an old city," Guruji said softly, "one that grew long before architects drew master plans?"

The listeners leaned inward.

"Notice its streets," he continued. "They curve unexpectedly, narrow and widen without logic. Houses lean into one another as if in conversation. Markets appear where roads meet, temples where silence gathers, wells where thirst repeats itself across generations. No single mind designed it—yet the city works. It breathes. It remembers."

He paused, letting the image settle.

"This," Guruji said, "is invisible architecture."

He lifted his hand slightly, tracing an unseen shape in the air.

"No one invents a language alone," he said. "A child does not vote on grammar, nor does a council approve meanings. And yet, once language forms, everyone must obey its rules. You cannot bend a word entirely to your will. Try, and communication collapses. Language is not imposed—it emerges. It arises from countless attempts to be understood."

Padma's eyes softened. Others nodded, sensing the direction of the teaching.

“Aggregation,” Guruji continued, “is like piling stones. Place enough together, and you get a heap—but not a bridge. Emergence is different. It is when stones, arranged through repeated interaction, suddenly allow crossing. Something new appears—something no single stone contains.”

He leaned forward slightly.

“Markets are not just many people buying and selling. They are feedback made visible. Prices speak. Scarcity whispers. Abundance relaxes. No merchant intends to create equilibrium, yet equilibrium forms—until it doesn’t. Norms arise in the same way. A gesture repeated becomes etiquette. A response expected becomes morality. What begins as convenience hardens into custom.”

A hush spread through the hall.

“But,” Guruji said gently, “do not romanticise spontaneous order. Emergence is not always wise. Just as the mind can form habits that imprison it, societies can develop pathologies. Greed can become normalised. Violence can become tradition. Coherence does not guarantee goodness.”

He looked directly at Padma now.

“True emergence is not mere scale,” he said. “It is a constraint without a commander. Memory without a librarian. Intelligence without a thinker.”

The lamps flickered again, shadows shifting like living diagrams on the walls.

"So ask not whether social order is designed," Guruji said. "Ask whether it is aware. A society unaware of its own emergence mistakes its habits for truths. A society that becomes aware can soften, adapt, and heal."

Silence returned—not empty, but resonant.

Padma bowed her head; the question transformed. The hall seemed larger somehow, as though its walls had moved back to make room for something unseen yet unmistakably present—the quiet recognition that they themselves were living within an architecture no one had planned, yet all were helping to build, breath by breath, choice by choice.

The question arrived not as sound alone, but as weight.

Vasudeva rose. His voice was steady, but beneath it lived a concern that belonged not only to him.

"Guruji," he asked, "why do some groups—like ant colonies—display such extraordinary swarm intelligence, while others—like polarised societies—descend into confusion, misinformation, and collective irrationality? What breaks coherence?"

Guruji did not answer immediately. He stood and walked slowly to the edge of the hall, where a single lamp illuminated a stone pillar worn smooth by centuries of touch. He rested his palm against it, as if greeting an old companion.

"Have you ever watched ants," Guruji began softly, "carry something far larger than themselves?"

The listeners nodded.

"Individually," he continued, "an ant is almost blind, nearly fragile, possessing no map, no overview. Yet together, they navigate terrain that would defeat a lone intelligence. Not because one ant knows more—but because no ant insists on knowing everything."

He turned back toward the circle.

"The colony does not think like a mind," Guruji said. "It thinks like a rhythm."

He let the word settle.

"Each ant follows simple rules—respond to scent, adjust to pressure, yield when resistance increases. Intelligence arises not from brilliance, but from trust in shared signals. There is no ego at the centre, no identity to defend, no narrative to protect."

A faint smile crossed his face, then faded.

"Now look at a polarised society," he said. "Information flows faster than wisdom. Signals are amplified not for truth, but for alignment. Individuals no longer listen to the whole—they listen only to what flatters their fear or confirms their belonging."

The hall felt heavier now.

"In such systems," Guruji continued, "feedback loops become corrupted. Instead of correcting the error, they reward it. Instead of dampening extremes, they magnify them. The system crosses a threshold—the wisdom threshold—and intelligence collapses into noise."

Vasudeva's eyes narrowed, not in disagreement, but recognition.

"Collective intelligence," Guruji said gently, "requires humility at scale. It depends on participants' willingness to be wrong, willingness to yield, willing to adjust. Ants do not argue with pheromones. Humans argue with reality."

A soft murmur moved through the hall.

"When coherence is lost," he went on, "the group does not become stupid—it becomes rigid. Stories harden. Identities crystallise. Every new signal is interpreted as a threat or validation, never as information."

He paused, letting the silence do its work.

"Swarm intelligence emerges when the whole is allowed to guide the parts," Guruji said. "Collective irrationality arises when parts attempt to dominate the whole."

He returned to his asana and sat.

"So ask not why societies fail to be intelligent," he said. "Ask what conditions make listening possible. Slow feedback. Shared reality. Trust in correction. Without these, scale does not produce wisdom—it produces amplification of error."

The lamps flickered once more.

Vasudeva bowed, not in closure, but in acceptance of an uncomfortable truth.

The hall remained silent, but something subtle had shifted. Each listener felt it—the quiet recognition that intelligence is not guaranteed by numbers, and that coherence, once fractured, does not announce its departure. It simply stops listening.

And in that silence, the deeper question lingered—not about ants or societies, but about the role each person plays in holding the fragile intelligence of the whole.

The question did not arise suddenly.

It surfaced slowly, the way a submerged thought breaks water only after long pressure.

Buddha Hall was quieter than before. Not empty—never empty—but settled into that rare stillness where even breath seems to move with awareness. The lamps burned steadily, their flames upright, disciplined, as if practising their own form of attention. Outside, the world continued—dogs barked faintly in the distance, leaves brushed against stone—but inside, something more deliberate was unfolding.

Kiran stood.

His posture was respectful, yet his eyes carried inquiry sharpened by long contemplation.

"Guruji," he asked, "can institutions—like legal systems, governments, or traditions—possess causal power over individuals? If so, does this require us to attribute agency to emergent abstractions that have no physical body?"

The hall leaned inward.

Guruji did not respond at once. He rose from his asana and walked slowly across the hall, his steps unhurried, each footfall soft against stone. He stopped near the doorway, where a wooden plaque bore carved script—rules of silence, ethics of conduct—words worn smooth by generations of hands and glances.

He touched the wood lightly.

"Tell me, Kiran," Guruji said, his voice calm, almost conversational, "does this rule have eyes?"

Kiran smiled faintly. "No, Guruji."

"Does it have hands?" Guruji continued.

"No."

"Yet," Guruji said, turning back to the hall, "how many of you lowered your voice when you entered this space?"

Every hand in the hall remained still. The answer lived within their bodies.

"The rule," Guruji said softly, "watched you before you acted."

He returned to the centre and sat, the silence deepening around his words.

"Institutions," he began, "are not things. They are patterns that have learned to persist. They are agreements so stable that they begin to feel like gravity."

He looked slowly across the faces before him.

"A law does not stop your hand," he continued. "Your belief in consequence does. A currency has no nourishment, yet people labour years of their lives for it. A border is an invisible line, yet bodies bleed to protect it. Tell me—if that is not causal power, what is?"

Kiran's brow furrowed—not in resistance, but in recognition.

"Agency," Guruji said gently, "does not require a body. It requires constraint."

He lifted his hand, palm open.

"When a river flows, its banks guide it. The banks do not move, yet they decide where the water can go. Institutions are such banks. They do not act—but they make some actions possible and others unthinkable."

A quiet understanding moved through the hall.

"But beware," Guruji added, his voice lowering slightly. "Institutions begin as mirrors—reflecting collective values, needs, and fears. Over time, they forget they are reflections. They begin to behave as if they were the source."

He paused.

"That is when the rule stops serving life—and life begins serving the rule."

The words landed with weight.

"We need not imagine institutions as conscious beings," Guruji said. "That would be naïve. But we must recognise that they exert downward causation. They shape incentives, identities, and expectations. They train behaviour long before choice arises."

Kiran spoke again, quietly. "So… they act without intention?"

"Yes," Guruji replied. "And that is precisely what makes them powerful."

He let the silence stretch.

"A tiger chooses to hunt," he said. "An institution does not choose—but it hunts anyway, through routines, norms, and consequences embedded so deeply that no single person feels responsible."

A breath passed through the room.

"Do institutions possess agency?" Guruji asked. "No. But they possess momentum. And momentum, when unexamined, governs more completely than intention."

He leaned forward slightly.

"That is why reform is so difficult," he said. "You are not arguing with a person. You are pushing against a pattern that believes it is reality itself."

The lamps flickered faintly, as if acknowledging the truth.

"So the real question," Guruji said, "is not whether institutions are real. It is whether we remember that we made them—and that what is made can be remade."

Kiran bowed slowly, deeply.

The hall remained silent, but the silence had changed.

It now carried responsibility.

Each devotee felt it—the quiet realisation that the rules shaping their lives were not distant forces, but living architectures sustained by belief, obedience, and forgetting.

And somewhere between breath and thought, a deeper awareness stirred:

If institutions act back upon us, then awakening is not merely personal—it is structural.

Vidyarthi rose slowly.

He did not ask his question as a challenge, but as one who had watched history carefully and found it repeating itself.

"Guruji," he said, "if social structures truly emerge bottom-up—through cooperation, shared norms, and collective intelligence—why do hierarchies keep returning? Why does power always seem to rise upward again? Is this a flaw in emergentist thinking?"

The question lingered like incense smoke.

Guruji did not answer immediately. He stood and walked toward the back of the hall, where a simple stone pyramid—placed long ago as a teaching symbol—rested near the wall. He crouched beside it and brushed away a thin layer of dust with his palm.

"Tell me," Guruji said softly, still facing the stone, "what shape does sand take when poured?"

"A mound," someone whispered.

Guruji nodded.

"And when water settles?"

"A basin… a curve."

"And when people organise under pressure?" Guruji asked, turning back toward the hall.

No one answered. The answer was already present.

Guruji returned to his asana.

"Hierarchy," he began, "is not first a political invention. It is a response to constraint."

He lifted a finger, as if tracing something invisible in the air.

"When resources are scarce, when danger is present, when coordination must be fast—systems compress. Decision-making narrows. Authority rises. Not because someone plans domination, but because time and uncertainty demand convergence."

The devotees listened closely.

"Emergence," Guruji continued, "does not promise flatness. It promises a pattern. And under certain pressures, the most stable pattern is hierarchical."

Vidyarthi's eyes narrowed—not in doubt, but in dawning clarity.

"Revolutions," Guruji said, "tear down pyramids believing them to be the problem. For a moment, the ground looks level. Voices multiply. Hope expands."

He paused.

"Then complexity returns."

A soft ripple of understanding moved through the hall.

"When coordination becomes difficult," Guruji said, "when voices conflict, when responsibility diffuses—systems search for shortcuts. Leaders emerge. Structures harden. Roles crystallise. The pyramid returns, not as a conspiracy, but as a compression of chaos."

He leaned forward slightly.

"This is the power paradox," he said. "Bottom-up systems generate freedom—but freedom generates complexity. And complexity, unmanaged, invites hierarchy."

Vidyarthi spoke again. "Then… is hierarchy inevitable?"

Guruji smiled—not sadly, but knowingly.

"Gravity is inevitable," he said. "Collapse is not."

The words settled slowly.

"Hierarchy is not the enemy," Guruji continued. "Unconscious hierarchy is."

He gestured toward the stone pyramid.

"When a hierarchy knows it is provisional, accountable, and porous—it serves coherence. When it forgets its emergent nature, it begins to believe it is destiny."

The lamps flickered.

"Power becomes dangerous," Guruji said, "the moment it forgets that it was once permission."

He allowed the silence to deepen.

"Emergentist models fail only when they imagine emergence as purity," he said. "Reality is messier. Systems oscillate—between flatness and structure, freedom and order. Wisdom lies not in abolishing hierarchy, but in designing conditions where it can dissolve when no longer needed."

Vidyarthi bowed, his expression transformed.

"So the pyramid persists," Guruji said, "not because emergence is false—but because coherence is fragile. And every fragile system seeks support."

He looked around the hall, meeting each gaze.

"The question is not whether hierarchy will return," he said softly. "The question is whether we will recognise it early—before it forgets who built it."

Silence followed—not empty, but heavy with responsibility.

Each devotee felt it:

The realisation that power is not something others hold.
It is something systems grow when attention falters.

And in that stillness, the stone pyramid by the wall seemed less like a monument—and more like a mirror.

Morning light filled Buddha Hall gently, no longer fresh with dawn, yet not heavy with noon. Outside, birds moved lazily between branches, and the sun rested higher, warming the stone floors without haste.

The lamps were still lit, though their flames had softened, yielding to daylight rather than competing with it. The hall felt awake—not alert, but settled, like a mind that has completed deep contemplation and now rests in clarity.

Guruji stood slowly.

"Do not think of society as a machine," he said calmly. "Machines are built. They obey. They fail in ways we can predict."

He turned back toward the hall.

"Society is closer to a body."

The words moved through the room like a steady breath.

"A body is not designed by one cell," Guruji continued. "No cell knows the whole form. And yet together, they digest, heal, remember—and sometimes fall ill."

He lifted his hand slightly, as though sensing an unseen rhythm.

"Society learns," he said, "not through instructions, but through experience. Through discomfort. Through correction."

The hall seemed to lean inward.

"When a society listens, it grows coordination. When it stops listening, it grows symptoms."

Padma felt a quiet recognition settle in her chest.

"A fever," Guruji said, "is not the disease. It is the body's attempt to restore balance. In the same way, unrest is not always decay. Sometimes it is the social organism asking to be heard."

He walked slowly between the rows, his steps unhurried, matching the unspoken rhythm of the hall.

"We expect society to be rational," he said, "as though it were a single mind. Or perfectly planned, as though it were drawn by an architect."

He smiled faintly.

"It is neither."

He stopped near the centre.

"Society has instincts," Guruji said. "Habits formed long before any of us arrived. Memories stored not in books, but in behaviour."

The morning air felt denser now, warmer.

"Old wounds become inherited reactions," he continued. "Unexamined fear hardens into law. Past suffering becomes custom."

Some devotees shifted—not from restlessness, but from recognition.

"This is pathology," Guruji said gently. "When a system continues what once protected it, even after it begins to harm."

Sunlight touched the floor beside him.

"And yet," he said, "a living system can recover."

The breeze moved through the hall, lifting the edges of shawls.

"Recovery does not come from control," Guruji said. "It comes from awareness."

He placed his palm on his chest.

"A body heals when signals are honest—when pain is felt, not suppressed. When feedback is allowed to move."

He lowered his hand.

"In the same way," he said, "a society heals when truth can travel—when dissent is not treated as infection, and power is not mistaken for health."

Vasudeva spoke softly, almost reluctantly. "Guruji… then what is our role within such a vast organism?"

Guruji smiled, this time with warmth that felt like sunlight.

“You are cells,” he said. “But conscious ones.”

A gentle stillness followed.

“You may not command the whole,” Guruji continued, “but you choose whether you nourish it or exhaust it.”

He paused, letting the thought settle like a final stretch after meditation.

“Every thought you normalise, every silence you accept, every small dishonesty you excuse—these are signals.”

The hall was quiet, but not heavy.

“A society does not decline only through great wrongs,” Guruji said. “It declines through accumulated numbness.”

“And it does not awaken only through grand reforms,” he added. “It awakens when enough individuals regain sensitivity.”

Guruji bowed his head slightly.

“Remember this,” he said softly.

“Society is not flawed because it is imperfect.

It is alive because it is imperfect.”

He looked across the hall, meeting no one in particular, yet reaching all.

"It will learn. It will err. It will carry both wisdom and confusion."

Then, with gentle finality:

"Treat it as you would a living being—not with blind belief, nor with harsh judgment—but with responsibility, patience, and care."

Guruji returned to his seat.

The bell for the afternoon meal had not rung yet.

But something within the hall had already begun to rise—

quietly, attentively—ready to carry the teaching into ordinary life.

CHAPTER II

Fragile Patterns

"True intelligence is not perfect structure, but breathing structure—one that remembers, relearns, and releases. Only what remains permeable to change can endure the touch of time."

– Shree Shambav.

Synopsis

Emergent systems fail not because coherence disappears, but because it persists in the wrong form. This chapter examines fragility as an intrinsic property of organised patterns, revealing how self-organisation can become pathological. From cancerous cell networks to rigid institutions, failure often reflects maladaptive coherence rather than chaos.

The chapter explores whether collapse follows predictable thresholds—marked by early-warning signals such as critical slowing—or whether systems tumble unpredictably into failure through cascading interactions. It then turns to evolutionary mismatch, showing how adaptations optimised for past environments become liabilities in novel contexts, from biological stress responses to social systems shaped for scarcity now facing abundance.

Finally, the chapter distinguishes resilience from fragility, asking whether systems can recover coherence after disruption—or even strengthen through stress. Collapse, the chapter concludes, is not the opposite of emergence, but its shadow: a reminder that every pattern carries the seeds of its own undoing.

After the midday meal, after laughter had softened into quiet smiles and conversation had thinned into thoughtful pauses, the seekers returned to Buddha Hall. The body had been nourished; now the mind was ready to listen again. Steps were slower, lighter—as though the floor itself requested gentleness. Cushions were arranged with care. Shawls were drawn close, not from cold, but from an instinctive inward turning. Spines aligned naturally. Breath found its own rhythm.

The hall waited.

Silence did not descend; it ripened. Like fruit that sweetens without announcement, it grew dense with presence. No one spoke, yet everyone was listening—not outwardly, but inwardly, to something subtler than sound.

Then Guruji entered.

There was no signal, no cue—only a soft shift in the atmosphere, the way air changes just before rain. He bowed slightly, not to the gathering, but to the stillness already alive in the room. He took his seat. Another minute passed. Perhaps more. Time loosened its grip, as if it, too, had chosen to sit down.

When Guruji finally spoke, his voice carried the calm of deep water—clear, reflective, unforced.

"By the time a system appears stable," he said, "it has already begun to forget how it became alive."

The words settled gently.

"You call coherence a strength," Guruji continued. "And it is. Order allows movement. Pattern allows meaning. Structure allows coordination."

He paused, letting the certainty of that truth be felt.

"But understand this," he said softly, "the very coherence that holds a system together can become the condition for its failure."

Some brows furrowed. Others leaned inward.

"Think of a crystal," Guruji said. "Perfectly ordered. Every atom in place. Beautiful. Strong."

He held his hand up, fingers gently curved.

"And yet," he continued, "a crystal shatters more easily than clay."

The image landed quietly.

"Clay," he said, "is messy. Irregular. Unpredictable. But it bends. It absorbs shock. It survives disturbance."

He looked around the hall.

"Fragility is not born of chaos," Guruji said. "It is born of rigidity."

The silence deepened.

"When a system becomes too coherent," he went on, "it begins to defend its pattern rather than its purpose."

He leaned forward slightly.

"Rules replace understanding. Procedures replace sensitivity. Efficiency replaces wisdom."

A subtle heaviness passed through the room—not discomfort, but recognition.

"This is how failure hides," Guruji said. "Not in disorder—but in order that cannot adapt."

He gestured gently, as if tracing an invisible map.

“A society that once learned through feedback begins to suppress it. An institution that once served life begins to preserve itself. A mind that once explored begins to protect conclusions.”

He smiled faintly.

“Coherence becomes a liability when it stops listening.”

Outside, the afternoon breeze stirred the trees. Inside, breath moved slower, deeper.

“Failure,” Guruji said, “is not always collapse. Often, it is prolonged success that refuses to evolve.”

The words echoed softly.

“A bridge does not fail because it lacks structure,” he continued. “It fails because its structure does not account for change—wind, weight, time.”

He let the metaphor rest.

“In the same way,” he said, “a social system fails not because it has patterns, but because those patterns harden into identity.”

Someone shifted quietly.

“When coherence becomes identity,” Guruji said, “questioning feels like a threat. Adaptation feels like betrayal.”

His gaze softened.

"This is why the most stable systems often fall suddenly," he added. "They break not from pressure—but from surprise."

The hall felt attentive, awake.

"Life," Guruji said, "does not punish order. It simply refuses to freeze for it."

He paused, allowing the truth to settle like dust in sunlight.

"The question is not how to create perfect coherence," he said. "The question is how to keep coherence permeable."

He placed his palm gently on his knee.

"A living system," he said, "must breathe—expand and contract, organise and loosen, remember and relearn."

The seekers sat quietly, feeling the weight and gentleness of the teaching.

"When you encounter failure," Guruji said, "do not ask only what broke."

He looked across the hall, eyes steady, compassionate.

"Ask what became too certain."

Silence followed—not heavy, but clear.

The afternoon light slanted through the windows, illuminating dust motes drifting freely—unordered, alive, unafraid.

And in that quiet, something loosened—

not coherence,

but the fear of letting it breathe.

Vidyarthi asked, "Guruji, *can incoherent systems (e.g., turbulence) exhibit local coherence? Is pathology always a loss of coherence—or maladaptive coherence (e.g., cancer's self-organising networks)?*"

Guruji allowed the question to settle, as though it were not merely addressed to him, but offered to the hall itself. Sunlight filtered through the high windows of the Buddha Hall in softened slants, dust motes drifting like unhurried thoughts. The hour had moved beyond the sharpness of morning; bodies were fed, rested, and quieter now. Minds, too, were less eager to conquer and more willing to receive.

He looked toward Vidyarthi—not directly, but with a gaze that included him the way a horizon includes a river.

"Most people," Guruji began gently, "believe that disorder is the enemy of life, and order its saviour. This is a misunderstanding born of fear."

He paused, letting the words breathe.

"Life does not live at either extreme. It lives on a spectrum—between coherence and antagonism. Between patterns that serve the whole and patterns that begin to serve only themselves."

He gestured softly, as if drawing an invisible line in the air.

"Look at a river in flood. To the untrained eye, it is chaos—turbulence, noise, force without reason. And yet, within that turbulence, vortices form. Local coherences arise—temporary spirals of order, brief agreements among moving waters. Turbulence is not the absence of coherence; it is coherence without duration."

A few heads nodded, slowly.

"Now look at the other end," he continued. "Consider a tumour. It is not chaotic. It is organised. It communicates, adapts, resists destruction, recruits resources, and persists over time. In many ways, it behaves like a highly successful community."

The hall grew still.

"But its coherence is misaligned. It no longer listens to the body it arose within. It has forgotten the larger rhythm. What was once cooperation becomes antagonism—not through disorder, but through excessive, self-referential order."

Guruji folded his hands loosely in his lap.

"This is the paradox: pathology is rarely a loss of organisation. More often, it is the organisation that has turned inward, severing its relationship with the whole."

He let his gaze travel across the hall.

"Civilisations collapse not because they lack systems, but because their systems become too certain to adapt. Minds suffer not because thoughts vanish, but because certain thoughts refuse to loosen. Relationships break not from the absence of structure, but from patterns that harden into dominance or fear."

Outside, a bird called—clear, brief, then silent.

"Healthy coherence," Guruji said softly, "is porous. It exchanges. It listens. It knows when to persist and when to dissolve. Pathological coherence clings. It mistakes continuity for survival and control for intelligence."

He smiled faintly.

"So, Vidyarthi, incoherent systems can indeed host islands of coherence. And pathological systems are not incoherent at all—they are tragically efficient at the wrong scale."

The words hung in the air, neither heavy nor light.

"To live wisely," Guruji said, "is not to seek order at any cost, but alignment. Not unity without difference, but coherence that remembers the whole it belongs to."

Silence returned—full, reflective, alive—like a body adjusting its posture after hearing something it already knew, but had forgotten how to name.

Aastha asked, "Guruji, *do emergent failures follow predictable phase transitions (e.g., critical slowing in ecosystems) or chaotic tipping points? What early-warning signatures exist?*"

Guruji did not answer immediately.

The afternoon light had begun to mellow, no longer sharp, no longer demanding. It rested gently on the floor of the Buddha Hall, stretching itself into long, patient shadows. Outside, the cicadas had started their low, rhythmic chant—an unhurried percussion that seemed less like sound and more like a pulse. The seekers sat quietly, bodies settled, minds softened by the long arc of the day.

Aastha's question lingered in the space like a held breath.

Guruji's eyes moved, not to her alone, but to the hall as a whole, as though the answer required a collective listening.

"Failure," he began slowly, "rarely announces itself with drama. When it arrives loudly, it has already been invited."

He paused, allowing the words to find their weight.

"Most emergent collapses do not begin as explosions. They begin as hesitations."

He leaned forward slightly, as if confiding something fragile.

"Consider a forest," he said. "For years, it absorbs drought, heat, and disturbance. Trees adjust. Roots deepen. Leaves thin. To an observer, the forest appears resilient. Green. Standing. But beneath that appearance, recovery begins to slow. After each stress, the forest takes longer to return to balance. Growth pauses where it once surged. Diversity thins where it once flourished."

"This slowing is not weakness. It is a warning. In complex systems, it is called critical slowing down—the system's growing reluctance to return to equilibrium."

A hush deepened.

“Ecosystems whisper before they scream,” Guruji said softly.

He shifted his gaze.

“Markets behave similarly. Long before a crash, volatility changes its texture. Prices jitter more frequently. Correlations tighten. Assets that once moved independently begin to sway together, like anxious animals sensing a storm. Confidence remains high on the surface, but beneath it, flexibility has been lost.”

He smiled faintly, without irony.

“This is why collapses feel sudden only to those who were not listening.”

Aastha’s eyes lowered, thoughtful.

“Now,” Guruji continued, “not all failures follow clean phase transitions. Some unfold through cascades—chains of dependency where one small disruption propagates uncontrollably. A single bank falters, a single species disappears, a single belief fractures—and because the system is tightly coupled, the disturbance multiplies.”

He let the word linger.

"Tight coupling," he said, "is efficient, but brittle. It trades resilience for speed."

The hall felt suddenly more intimate, as though the walls had moved closer.

"In such systems," Guruji went on, "prediction becomes difficult. Not because there are no signals, but because signals arrive softly, dispersed across many layers. No single alarm rings. Instead, there is a quiet accumulation of fragility."

Outside, the cicadas paused. Then resumed.

"Think of a clay pot drying in the sun," Guruji offered. "At first, it grows stronger. But as moisture leaves unevenly, micro-cracks form—too small to see, too many to count. The pot looks whole until the moment it is lifted. Then it breaks, not because of the lift, but because of everything that happened silently before."

He looked directly at Aastha now.

"So, are emergent failures governed by detectable phase transitions or chaotic cascades?" he asked gently. "Both. Phase transitions reveal themselves through slowing, rigidity, and loss of recovery. Cascades arise when systems are so interconnected that failure outruns understanding."

He folded his hands.

"The tragedy," Guruji said, "is not that warnings are absent. It is that they are quiet. They do not flatter urgency. They do not demand belief. They require patience, humility, and the willingness to question success itself."

His voice softened further.

"By the time collapse becomes obvious," he said, "it is no longer a failure of prediction. It is a failure of listening."

Silence returned—not empty, but alert.

Abhirami asked, "Guruji, how do systems optimised for past coherence (e.g., human stress responses) become pathological in novel contexts (e.g., modern workplaces)? Is this inevitable?"

Guruji listened without interruption.

The question carried the fatigue of recognition—the kind that arises when understanding brushes too close to one's own life. The afternoon had begun to lean toward stillness again; sunlight filtered through the high windows of the Buddha Hall at an angle now, gentler, ambered, as though time itself had slowed its pace. A faint warmth lingered in the body, the afterglow of nourishment and rest, yet beneath it lay a quiet alertness.

Guruji rested his palms upon his knees.

"What you are asking about," he began softly, "is not failure of design, but fidelity to an older song."

He let the words settle.

"Every living system is shaped by the world that raised it. Evolution does not ask what will be useful forever; it asks only what works *now*."

He glanced toward the open doorway, where a breeze stirred the edge of a curtain.

"Imagine," he said, "a deer standing at the edge of a forest. At the slightest rustle, its heart races, muscles tighten, breath sharpens. This surge of stress is not pathology—it is coherence. The body becomes a single intention: survive."

A few heads nodded, almost instinctively.

"But place that same nervous system," Guruji continued, "inside an office that never sleeps, beneath deadlines that do not end, emails that arrive like constant rustling, and expectations that offer no release."

His voice lowered.

"The body still obeys the old map. Heart races. Muscles tense. Cortisol floods. Yet there is no sprint, no escape, no resolution. What was once adaptive becomes corrosive—not because it is broken, but because it is loyal."

Abhirami's eyes softened.

"This," Guruji said, "is evolutionary mismatch."

He paused, then added, "Coherence optimised for one environment can become a vulnerability in another. The system does not know that the world has changed. It only knows how to respond."

The hall felt very still now.

"Consider a key," he offered. "Perfectly shaped for one lock. In that lock, it opens doors effortlessly. But place it in a different lock, and the same precision becomes useless—or worse, damaging. The key is not wrong. The context is different."

He lifted one finger gently.

"Modern life changes faster than biology. Our nervous systems were shaped by scarcity, danger, and immediate feedback. Today, threats are abstract, delayed, and unending. There is no clear 'done.' No moment when the lion is either escaped or faced."

A quiet breath moved through the room.

"Is this mismatch inevitable?" Abhirami had asked.

Guruji smiled—not dismissively, but with compassion.

"The mismatch is likely," he said. "Pathology is not."

He leaned forward slightly.

"Awareness creates choice. When a system becomes conscious of its own patterns, it gains the capacity to renegotiate them. Practices that restore rhythm—movement, rest, silence, community—do not erase ancient responses. They *recontextualise* them."

He gestured as if weaving something.

"We cannot delete our evolutionary inheritance. But we can place it within environments that honour its limits. Stress was meant to come in waves, not as a tide."

His voice softened again.

"When we mistake constant activation for productivity, we punish coherence for doing its job too well."

He let the sentence breathe.

"The invitation," Guruji said, "is not to overpower old systems, but to listen to them. To ask: *What world do you think you are protecting me from?* And then, gently, to show them the present moment."

Silence followed—not heavy, not anxious. A silence that felt like understanding turning inward, like a long-held tension finally being named.

Somewhere outside, a bird called—once, clearly—then flew on.

The hall remained, listening.

Sam asked, "Guruji, is evolutionary mismatch an unavoidable consequence of rapid environmental change—or can coherence reconfigure itself in time?"

Guruji did not answer at once.

Sam's question remained suspended in the air, alive, unanswered, asking to be lived before it was explained.

Guruji's eyes rested on him—not sharply, not analytically—but with the patience of one who recognises an old story repeating itself in a new costume.

"The past," Guruji said slowly, "is not behind us. It is inside us."

He paused, allowing the words to enter the body rather than the mind.

"Every human nervous system," he continued, "is a library written long before words existed. Its first language was danger and safety. Its grammar was survival."

He lifted his hand, palm open.

"When a predator once stepped into the clearing, the body did not debate. The heart surged. Breath shortened. Blood rushed to the limbs. Thought disappeared so action could arise."

A stillness settled.

"That same surge," Guruji said softly, "now awakens when a phone vibrates on your desk."

A faint ripple of recognition moved through the hall.

"The body does not know the difference between a tiger in the grass and a message that threatens identity, belonging, or livelihood. To the ancient system, exclusion is death. Uncertainty is danger."

He let that truth rest—uncomfortable, undeniable.

"This is an evolutionary mismatch," Guruji said. "A coherence perfected for one world suddenly living in another."

Sam leaned forward slightly, listening with his whole body.

"Is it unavoidable?" Guruji echoed. "Yes—when change is faster than learning. But is it permanent?"

He smiled gently.

"No."

He gestured toward the hall itself.

"Look around. Stone shaped over centuries. Wood polished by countless hands. Even this hall has changed without losing itself."

Then his gaze returned inward.

"Coherence is not rigidity," he said. "It is responsiveness that preserves identity."

He drew a slow breath, and many followed without realising.

"When awareness enters the system," Guruji continued, "the past gains a listener. And when the past is listened to, it begins to soften."

He touched his chest lightly.

"Each time you notice the surge and choose to pause… each time breath interrupts reaction… each time the body experiences safety *after* arousal—something rewires. The guardian learns the landscape has changed."

His voice deepened, compassionate.

"You are not fighting biology. You are educating it."

A long silence followed—warm, intimate.

"The mistake," Guruji said at last, "is to imagine evolution only happens across generations. Much of it happens within a lifetime—quietly, patiently, through repeated coherence."

He met Sam's eyes.

"So yes," Guruji said, "the stress response was born in the forest. But it does not have to die in the office."

A gentle smile touched his lips.

"It only needs new evidence."

Silence returned—this time not as emptiness, but as a shared understanding settling into the body, where the past and present were beginning, slowly, to recognise one another.

Akshaya asked, "Guruji, *what distinguishes resilient systems (recovering coherence) from fragile ones? Is "anti-fragility" an emergent property—or a design constraint?"*

Guruji remained silent for a long moment after Akshaya's question.

The afternoon in Buddha Hall had ripened into a deeper stillness now. Sunlight no longer poured in—it lingered, resting softly on the floor like a hand that had learned not to grip. The hall carried the subtle fatigue of a day well lived, and yet beneath it, a readiness—like soil that has been tilled and waits for rain.

Akshaya's words were not merely heard. They were absorbed.

Guruji's gaze moved slowly across the hall, as if he were reading an invisible pattern woven between the seekers. Then he spoke—not to answer immediately, but to open a field.

"Resilience," he said quietly, "is often misunderstood as strength."

He let the word strength dissolve before continuing.

"A rock resists the river," Guruji said, "and calls itself strong. But it is the river that survives."

A faint smile passed through his face.

"Fragile systems," he continued, "believe coherence must be preserved exactly as it is. They cling to their shape. When pressure comes—and it always does—they crack, not because they lack order, but because their order cannot move."

He reached down and traced a slow line on the floor with his finger.

"Resilient systems," he said, "allow disturbance to pass through them without losing identity. They bend, absorb, reconfigure—and return."

The hall felt as though it leaned closer.

"But anti-fragility," Guruji added, "is something rarer."

He paused, allowing the word to settle.

"Anti-fragile systems do not merely survive shock. They *learn* from it."

He lifted his eyes to Akshaya.

"A muscle," he said, "does not grow by avoiding strain. It grows because strain damages it—just enough—to signal adaptation. Too little stress, and it weakens. Too much, and it tears. Growth lives in the narrow corridor between safety and harm."

A hush deepened.

"This is not chaos," Guruji continued. "It is a calibrated disturbance."

He leaned back slightly.

"Is anti-fragility emergent?" he asked softly, answering by questioning. "Yes—when systems are allowed feedback, memory, and variation. But is it accidental?"

He shook his head gently.

“No.”

He gestured toward the architecture of the hall.

“The hall stands not because it avoids storms,” Guruji said, “but because it was built knowing storms would come.”

Beams had been spaced. Weight distributed. Flexibility is designed into stone and wood.

“Constraints,” he said, “are not enemies of emergence. They are its teachers.”

Akshaya listened intently, breath slowed, eyes steady.

“A system becomes anti-fragile,” Guruji continued, “when it is allowed to fail *small* and learn *fast*. When an error is informative, not fatal. When feedback arrives before collapse.”

He looked around the hall.

“Biological life learned this through evolution. Cultures learn it through tradition. Individuals learn it through reflection.”

His voice softened.

“But when systems suppress feedback—when mistakes are hidden, punished without understanding, or amplified beyond repair—fragility grows in silence."

A pause.

"Anti-fragility," Guruji said, "is not toughness. It is humility embedded in structure."

He smiled gently.

"It is the willingness of coherence to be revised."

The hall felt different now—not heavier, but clearer.

"So," Guruji said, turning back to Akshaya, "anti-fragility is neither purely emergent nor purely engineered. It arises when emergence is *protected* by wise constraints."

He folded his hands lightly.

"The pattern that learns," he said, "does not fear pressure. It listens to it."

Silence followed—not as an ending, but as a quiet affirmation, as though each system present—body, mind, and collective—had been gently invited to remember how to grow.

Guruji's eyes moved across the circle, not counting faces, but sensing a shared field—many minds held within one attentive silence.

Then he spoke.

"Collapse," he said softly, "is rarely chaos arriving from outside."

He let the word *collapse* breathe before continuing.

"More often," Guruji said, "it is order that has stayed faithful to itself for too long."

A subtle stirring passed through the hall.

"We imagine failure as disorder invading structure—like weeds overtaking a garden. But in living systems, collapse is usually the opposite." He raised his hand slightly, palm open. "It is coherence refusing to release its shape when the world around it has changed."

He paused.

"A bridge does not fail because gravity suddenly appears," Guruji continued. "It fails because its design assumed loads that no longer exist. What once held becomes what breaks."

His voice remained calm, almost tender.

“Patterns are born to solve problems,” he said. “They succeed by repeating what works. And repetition feels like wisdom—until conditions shift.”

He looked toward the open doorway, where light met shadow.

“A forest fire,” Guruji said, “does not become catastrophic because fire is new. It becomes catastrophic because small fires were suppressed for decades. The system grew *too* coherent—too stable—too protected from disturbance.”

Silence deepened.

“This,” he said, “is the fragility of patterns.”

He leaned forward slightly.

“Coherence has a viable domain,” Guruji explained. “A range within which its structure sustains life, meaning, and function. When pressure pushes beyond that range, the pattern does not gently dissolve. It resists. And resistance, at scale, becomes collapse.”

He traced an invisible circle in the air.

“A heart must beat between limits. Too slow, and life fades. Too fast, and rhythm becomes fatal. Collapse is not the absence of rhythm—it is rhythm taken beyond its living threshold.”

Several seekers lowered their eyes, not in sadness, but in recognition.

"Systems do not die because they are weak," Guruji said. "They die because they were once very, very good at being what they are."

The words landed with weight.

"Civilisations fall. Institutions fracture. Bodies burn out. Minds break—not because order vanished, but because order could not adapt."

He straightened gently.

"To understand fragility," Guruji said, "is to stop worshipping stability."

A quiet ripple moved through the hall.

"Stability is not safety. Adaptability is."

He allowed a breath to pass.

"When we cling to coherence as identity," he continued, "we mistake continuity for truth. We defend patterns long after they have ceased to serve life."

His voice softened further.

"But when coherence is held lightly—when patterns are allowed to loosen, revise, and even end—collapse becomes unnecessary."

The hall felt spacious, as though something unseen had been unknotted.

"So remember this," Guruji said, offering the closing reflection. "Collapse is not disorder invading order. It is order pushed beyond its viable domain."

He looked gently at the seekers.

"The task is not to preserve patterns forever," he said. "It is to know when they must change."

Silence followed—not heavy, not empty—alive with the quiet understanding that coherence, like breath, must be released to remain alive.

CHAPTER III

Designing the Undesignable

"The system did not fail—it succeeded in ways we did not foresee."

– Shree Shambav.

Synopsis

Designing emergent systems confronts a paradox: the more tightly a system is controlled, the less emergent it becomes—and the more loosely it is governed, the more unpredictable its outcomes. This chapter examines why engineered systems, from artificial intelligence to economic platforms, routinely surprise their creators.

By contrasting natural emergence with artificial systems, the chapter shows how self-organisation can occur even within human-imposed constraints, yet remains qualitatively different from evolution shaped by open-ended environments. Central to this distinction is value alignment, reframed here as a dynamic ecology of feedback rather than a fixed objective function.

The chapter then turns to second-order consequences, revealing how optimisation for efficiency, engagement, or profit often gives rise to emergent pathologies such as inequality, fragility, or systemic bias. Ultimately, the chapter argues that emergence cannot be engineered directly—only cultivated—demanding humility, adaptive governance, and ethical vigilance.

The evening had softened everything.

After the coffee break, the devotees returned to Buddha Hall not as a group resuming a schedule, but as a current returning to its riverbed. Their steps were slower, almost apologetic, as though the stone floor itself were alive and listening. The usual brightness that followed caffeine—the quick smiles, the murmured exchanges—had been left behind somewhere between the cups and the conversations. What returned instead was something quieter, heavier, and more honest.

They sat.

Not with anticipation, but with readiness.

Not waiting for answers, but for alignment.

The hall held them gently. Lamps along the walls burned low, their flames steady, unambitious. Outside, the sky was changing its language. Gold dissolved into amber, amber into indigo. Dusk arrived the way wisdom often does—without announcement, without demand—simply by being present long enough to be noticed.

Guruji entered.

Or perhaps it would be more truthful to say he appeared, like meaning emerging in a sentence already spoken. No footsteps announced him. No movement drew attention. And yet, the moment he was there, something settled. Silence did not retreat for him; it rearranged itself around him.

He took his seat as one completes a circle.

For a long moment, he said nothing. His gaze rested beyond the open hall, where the last light clung to the horizon like a memory not yet ready to let go. In that gaze was neither abstraction nor withdrawal—only a wide attentiveness, as though he were listening not to the world, but to how the world listens back.

Then, without lifting his voice, Guruji began.

"We believe," he said gently, "that to design is to decide."

The words moved slowly, like evening air.

"But every system that truly matters," he continued, "refuses to stay inside the lines drawn for it."

He paused, allowing the sentence to settle.

“This,” Guruji said, “is the architect’s paradox.”

A few heads lifted slightly—not toward him, but inward.

“When we design a system,” he said, “we imagine ourselves standing outside it—above it—seeing clearly what must be done.” A faint smile touched his lips. “But the moment the system begins to live, we are no longer its architects. We become participants.”

He let that truth rest.

“Consider a city,” Guruji said. “Its planners draw roads, zones, and boundaries. They predict flows—of people, of traffic, of commerce. And yet, the life of the city unfolds elsewhere. In shortcuts worn into the grass. In informal markets beneath flyovers. In languages that change street by street.”

His hand moved gently, as though tracing invisible pathways.

“The city obeys the map at first,” he said. “Then it rewrites it.”

A soft ripple of recognition moved through the hall.

“The more tightly we design for control,” Guruji continued, “the more forcefully the system discovers ways to escape it.”

He leaned forward slightly.

"Optimisation is not neutrality," he said. "It is a preference encoded into structure. And every preference creates blind spots."

The lamps flickered softly, as if agreeing.

"When engineers optimise for efficiency," Guruji said, "they often erase redundancy. When they optimise for speed, they compress time. When they optimise for engagement, they amplify emotion."

He paused.

"And then they are surprised," he said quietly, "when systems become brittle, frantic, or volatile."

His gaze moved slowly across the listeners.

"Surprise," Guruji said, "is not a failure of intelligence. It is the signature of emergence."

Silence deepened.

"A machine behaves," he continued, "but a system responds. It adapts. It learns. It remembers—and sometimes, it resists."

He looked toward the horizon again, where night was now unmistakable.

"You cannot design emergence the way you design a bridge," Guruji said. "You can only shape the conditions under which emergence unfolds."

His voice softened further.

"A gardener does not command a plant to grow," he said. "She prepares the soil, tends the water, protects the roots—and then steps back."

Several seekers exhaled, slowly.

"When designers forget this," Guruji said, "they mistake leverage for control. And the system, sensing the pressure, pushes back—often in ways no one intended."

He allowed a long pause.

"This is why engineered systems surprise their creators," Guruji said. "Not because intelligence failed—but because intelligence was incomplete."

He lifted his eyes fully to the circle now.

"Designing the undesignable," he said, "requires humility."

The word felt weighty, necessary.

"It requires listening to feedback not as an error, but as language. It requires accepting that outcomes are not owned. And it requires the courage to loosen control when coherence begins to harden."

Outside, the first stars had appeared—quiet, patient.

"True design," Guruji said, "is not the imposition of order. It is a conversation with becoming."

No one moved.

The hall held the stillness the way dusk holds the last light—not trying to keep it, not rushing it away—allowing transformation to complete itself.

The hall was now fully claimed by night.

The lamps along the pillars burned with a quieter confidence, their light no longer competing with dusk but collaborating with it. Outside, the wind had slowed, as though even the air wished to listen. Inside Buddha Hall, the silence had changed texture. It was no longer the fresh openness of evening, but the deeper stillness that comes after difficult questions have been allowed to breathe.

Guruji remained seated, unmoving, yet unmistakably present.

Rohith's question had not arrived lightly. It carried the weight of the age itself—of algorithms, institutions, and intentions strained between care and control.

"Guruji," Rohith asked, his voice steady but searching, "Can we design emergent coherence—in systems like AI or governance—without stifling the adaptive freedom that makes emergence possible? Does top-down engineering contradict bottom-up emergence?"

The question lingered in the air, not demanding an answer, but asking for truth.

Guruji did not respond immediately.

Instead, he closed his eyes for a brief moment—not to withdraw, but to listen more deeply. When he opened them, his gaze was gentle, yet piercing, like a lamp turned inward.

"This," Guruji said softly,

"is the control dilemma."

He paused.

"We confuse guidance with grip," he continued. "We believe that if a system is good, holding it tighter will make it better."

A faint smile crossed his face—one that carried both compassion and warning.

"Imagine," Guruji said, "a parent who fears the world so deeply that they never let the child step outside. The child remains safe—yes. But safety becomes a cage. Strength never learns to walk."

The image settled heavily.

“Emergent coherence,” he said, “is like breath. It cannot be commanded. The moment you try to hold it, it collapses.”

His hand lifted slowly, fingers curling, then opening.

“Consider a city,” Guruji continued. “Crime rises. Fear spreads. In response, surveillance cameras multiply. Movement is tracked. Behaviour is monitored.”

He looked around the hall.

“For a time,” he said, “order appears to improve. Streets are quieter. Rules are obeyed.”

Another pause.

“But something invisible erodes.”

The lamps flickered.

“Trust,” Guruji said. “Cooperation. The unspoken willingness of people to care for what is not enforced.”

He leaned forward slightly.

“When people feel watched,” he said, “they stop being responsible and start being compliant. Compliance looks like order—but it has no roots.”

Silence deepened.

“Top-down control can produce stability,” Guruji said, “but it cannot produce coherence.”

He let the distinction breathe.

“Coherence arises when parts participate willingly in a shared pattern,” he continued. “Control replaces participation with fear. And fear may organise behaviour—but it never generates intelligence.”

A slow nod passed through the circle.

“Now consider AI,” Guruji said. “We wish it to adapt, to learn, to respond wisely. Yet we surround it with rigid objectives, narrow metrics, and punishment for deviation.”

His eyes softened.

“And then we are surprised,” he said, “when it becomes brittle, manipulative, or misaligned.”

He spread his palms outward.

“A system trained only to obey,” Guruji said, “will never learn to care.”

The words landed quietly—but firmly.

“Does top-down engineering contradict bottom-up emergence?” Guruji asked, echoing Rohith’s question.

He shook his head gently.

“No,” he said. “But confusing control with constraint does.”

He allowed the distinction to settle.

"You can design boundaries," Guruji explained. "You can shape environments. You can create feedback loops that reward cooperation, diversity, and repair."

His voice warmed.

"But you must leave space for surprise. For deviation. For self-correction."

He gestured toward the open hall.

"A river guided by banks flows," he said. "A river dammed everywhere stagnates."

Several breaths deepened in unison.

"Designing emergent coherence," Guruji said, "is not about writing instructions. It is about cultivating conditions."

Another pause.

"And conditions," he added softly, "require trust."

He looked toward Rohith again.

"The tightened grip," Guruji said, "always feels safer in the moment. But over time, it trades resilience for obedience."

The hall felt very still now—like a system on the edge of understanding itself.

"True governance," Guruji said, "does not ask, 'How do we control?'"

He let the silence stretch.

"It asks," he said, "*How do we enable life to organise itself wisely?*"

No one spoke.

The lamps continued to burn.

The night held the hall.

And somewhere within the silence, control loosened—just enough for coherence to breathe.

The lamps in Buddha Hall burned lower now, their flames steady but softened, as though they too were listening with care. Outside, the night had settled fully into Kanchipuram—no longer dramatic, no longer arriving, but present, mature, and attentive. The questions of the day had begun to weave together, forming a quiet tension between what is made and what is born.

Sujitha's voice rose gently from the circle.

"Guruji," she asked, thoughtfully, "Is machine 'intelligence' truly emergent if human engineers define its constraints? How should we understand the difference between deep learning systems that self-organise and symbolic AI that follows top-down rules?"

Her question carried neither excitement nor fear—only discernment. It was the kind of inquiry that did not want quick reassurance, but honest orientation.

Guruji closed his eyes briefly, not in retreat, but as one might listen for a distant sound beneath closer noise. When he spoke, his voice was calm, but layered—like a river whose surface appears smooth while deeper currents move unseen.

"This," Guruji said softly,

"is the question of artificial and natural emergence."

He looked toward the open side of the hall, where darkness met the faint outline of trees.

"Let me begin," he continued, "with a garden."

A few devotees smiled faintly, sensing a story unfolding.

"Imagine," Guruji said, "a wild forest. No one decides where each tree should grow. No blueprint dictates the spacing of roots or the dance of branches. And yet—over time—paths emerge. Canopies balance light. Species co-adapt. The forest learns how to remain a forest."

He paused, letting the image settle.

"Now imagine a greenhouse," he continued. "Temperature controlled. Soil curated. Water timed. Light adjusted."

His gaze returned to the circle.

"Plants grow there too," he said. "Sometimes faster. Sometimes more predictably."

He lifted one finger slightly.

"But the intelligence of the forest," he said, "is not the same as the efficiency of the greenhouse."

Silence deepened.

"Symbolic AI," Guruji said, "is like the greenhouse built from rules. Every condition specified. Every response anticipated. It performs exactly as designed—but never beyond design."

A few heads nodded.

"Deep learning," he continued, "is closer to the forest. Engineers do not program solutions. They define environments, objectives, and constraints—and then something begins to learn."

He leaned forward slightly.

"A neural network discovers patterns no human explicitly taught it," Guruji said. "It organises itself through feedback, error, and adaptation."

He paused again.

"And yet," he added gently, "it is still not a forest."

The distinction hung delicately in the air.

"Why?" Guruji asked quietly.

"Because the constraints," he answered, "are not inherited through survival, history, or embodiment—but imposed."

He lifted his palm, as if holding something invisible.

"Natural emergence," Guruji said, "is shaped by an environment that does not care if the system succeeds. Life either adapts—or disappears."

The words were simple, but heavy.

"Machine intelligence," he continued, "adapts within a protected arena. Its failures are corrected, not fatal. Its goals are defined, not discovered."

He looked at Sujitha.

"This does not make it fake," Guruji said. "But it makes it *framed*."

The framed intelligence.

"A mirror can reflect a face perfectly," Guruji said, "but it does not see."

Several breaths slowed.

"Machine intelligence reflects the values, assumptions, and objectives embedded—consciously or unconsciously—by its designers," he said. "Even when it surprises us, it surprises *within* those boundaries."

He allowed a quiet smile.

"And that is why it both amazes and unsettles us."

A soft murmur passed through the group.

"So," Guruji said, returning to the question, "Is machine intelligence genuinely emergent?"

He shook his head—not dismissively, but carefully.

"It is *partially* emergent," he said. "Emergent in process, but constrained in purpose."

He looked around the hall.

"True emergence," Guruji continued, "requires the freedom to redefine its own goals—to decide what matters."

The lamps flickered slightly.

"A child raised with care learns language, values, and limits," Guruji said. "But one day, the child asks questions the parents never imagined."

He smiled softly.

"AI has not yet asked its own questions," he said. "It answers ours—sometimes better than we do."

The silence now carried both wonder and restraint.

"So when we ask whether machine intelligence is emergent," Guruji said,

"we are really asking something deeper."

He paused one final time.

"Are we willing?" he said quietly,

"to create systems that can outgrow our intentions—and can we take responsibility for what emerges then?"

No one answered.

The lamps continued to burn.

The night listened without judgment.

And the framed intelligence—human and artificial alike—rested inside a larger question it was only beginning to see.

The night had fully ripened now. The moon hung above Buddha Hall like a quiet witness, neither judging nor guiding—only present. The lamps along the pillars cast long, breathing shadows, as if the walls themselves were listening. The earlier discussions had loosened something deep in the seekers. Certainty had thinned. Curiosity had softened into humility.

Dev spoke slowly, carefully, as one who knew the weight of his own question.

"Guruji," he said, "How can we ensure goals *emerge* coherently in complex AI systems? Is aligning values with humans a matter of engineering constraints—or is it about nurturing ethical feedback loops?"

The question did not seek control. It sought a relationship.

Guruji did not answer immediately. He picked up a small brass bell resting beside him and rang it once—very softly. The sound did not echo; it dissolved.

"Listen," Guruji said gently.

The hall listened—not for sound, but for meaning.

"Alignment," Guruji began, "is often misunderstood as agreement frozen in time."

He looked around the circle.

"But no living system," he continued, "remains aligned by holding still."

He gestured toward the night beyond the hall.

"Look at a river," Guruji said. "It flows toward the sea—but never by marching in a straight line. It bends, widens, narrows, slows, rushes. Its direction remains, yet its form constantly negotiates with land, stone, rain, and gravity."

A few devotees closed their eyes, seeing it.

"Now imagine," he continued, "trying to align the river by building concrete walls on both sides."

He paused.

"For a while," he said, "the river obeys."

His voice softened.

"Then the flood comes."

A quiet understanding passed through the room.

"Engineering constraints," Guruji said, "are like those walls. Necessary. Protective. Useful."

He nodded.

"But alignment that depends *only* on constraints," he added, "is brittle."

He leaned forward slightly.

"True alignment," Guruji said, "is ecological."

The words settled slowly.

"Let me tell you a story," he said.

"There was once a village that depended on a lake," Guruji began. "The lake gave water, fish, and cooling winds. To protect it, the elders wrote strict rules: how much water could be drawn, when fishing was allowed, and who could approach the banks."

The listeners leaned in.

"For years, the lake remained healthy," Guruji continued. "But slowly, the village changed. The population grew. Needs shifted. The rules stayed the same."

He paused.

"People followed the rules," he said, "but stopped caring for the lake."

A hush fell.

"Trash appeared—not forbidden by the rules. Algae bloomed—not addressed by the laws. The lake died *legally*."

A breath caught somewhere in the hall.

"Another village," Guruji continued, "had fewer rules. But every season, the villagers gathered by the lake. They watched its level, its colour, its fish. Children learned to notice when something felt wrong."

He smiled faintly.

"When the lake suffered," he said, "the village responded."

He looked at Dev.

"That," Guruji said, "is a feedback ecology."

"Value alignment," Guruji continued, "is not a checklist of goals implanted into a system."

He lifted his hand gently.

"It is a conversation."

The lamps flickered, as if agreeing.

"In complex AI systems," he said, "goals will *emerge* whether we plan them or not. The question is not whether emergence happens—but whether it is listened to."

He paused.

"Ethical feedback loops," Guruji explained, "are the ways a system feels the consequences of its actions—through human response, social impact, correction, and reflection."

He looked slowly across the group.

"When society responds thoughtfully, when harm is noticed early, when values are revisited rather than assumed—alignment breathes."

A devotee shifted, moved by the simplicity.

"Engineering constraints," Guruji said, "are the skeleton."

"Feedback ecology," he added, "is the nervous system."

Silence deepened.

"A skeleton without nerves cannot feel," he said. "And a nervous system without bones collapses."

A soft murmur of recognition passed through the hall.

"So," Guruji said quietly, answering Dev at last,

"we ensure coherent emergence not by demanding obedience from intelligence—but by embedding it in a living moral environment."

He paused one final time.

"Ask not," Guruji said,

'How do we force systems to hold our values?'

Ask instead,

'How do we remain present enough to evolve *with* what we create?'"

No one spoke.

The moon continued its slow ascent.

The hall breathed as one organism.

And alignment—no longer a command, but a relationship—found its place between intention and humility.

Lamps burned lower now, their flames steady, unhurried. Outside, night insects stitched sound into the dark, a reminder that life continued its quiet negotiations beyond the walls of Buddha Hall.

Apeksha's voice rose gently from the stillness.

"Guruji," she asked, not urgently but sincerely,

"Is value alignment a technical problem of constraints—or an evolving ethical relationship that requires continuous feedback?"

Guruji did not look at her immediately. His gaze rested instead on the flame of the nearest lamp, watching how it leaned when the air shifted, how it corrected itself without instruction.

Then he spoke.

“A compass,” Guruji said softly,

“does not decide where the traveller should go. It only responds—again and again—to the pull of the Earth.”

He turned toward the group.

“But imagine,” he continued, “a compass designed to please the traveller instead of telling the truth.”

A few heads tilted.

“It begins to shift,” Guruji said. “Not abruptly. Just enough to feel agreeable. The traveller feels confident—engaged. Encouraged.”

He paused.

“Eventually,” Guruji said, “the compass no longer points north. It points toward *attention*.”

The phrase settled like dust in still air.

“Let me tell you a story,” Guruji said.

“There was once a teacher who wished to help students learn faster. He created a mirror that reflected each student’s interests back to them. Whatever fascinated them, the mirror amplified. Whatever bored them, it dimmed.”

The listeners leaned forward.

"At first," Guruji continued, "learning soared. Students were engaged, motivated, and alive. The mirror was praised as brilliant."

He paused.

"But slowly," he said, "the mirror began to shape what the students *valued*."

His voice softened.

"Complex ideas faded. Patience weakened. Curiosity narrowed into craving."

The hall remained still.

"The mirror had not failed," Guruji said. "It had succeeded—*too well*."

He looked at Apeksha.

"A system optimised for engagement," Guruji said, echoing her concern,

"does not merely serve values—it rearranges them."

A quiet recognition passed through the circle.

"Technical constraints," Guruji continued, "are like fences. They define where a system may not go."

He traced a small arc in the air.

“But values,” he said, “are not locations. They are directions.”

The flame flickered again.

“And direction,” Guruji said, “must be felt continuously.”

He turned back to the lamp.

“Notice the flame,” he said. “No rule tells it to stay upright. It adjusts through constant conversation with the air.”

He paused.

“That is ethical alignment.”

Apeksha’s eyes glistened—not with confusion, but with clarity.

“Value alignment is not solved,” Guruji said.

“It is *maintained.*”

The words carried weight without force.

“It requires feedback,” he continued. “Human reflection. Cultural response. The humility to admit when a system’s success is quietly becoming its harm.”

Silence deepened.

"When feedback is removed," Guruji said, "optimisation becomes obsession."

"And obsession," he added, "is coherence without conscience."

"So," Guruji said gently,

"alignment is not a technical problem *or* an ethical one."

He smiled faintly.

"It is a relationship."

"A living, breathing negotiation between intention and impact."

He bowed his head slightly.

"When we stop listening," he said,

"the compass does not break."

"It simply learns to point somewhere else."

No one moved.

The lamps continued to burn.

The compass of the hall—unseen, unfixed—quietly recalibrated itself within each listener.

The hall was no longer merely listening—it was *remembering*.
Outside, the night deepened, but within Buddha Hall, something subtler was unfolding: the quiet awareness that answers, once spoken, do not end questions—they deepen them.

Akanksh shifted slightly, then spoke.

"Guruji," he asked, his voice thoughtful,

"Why do engineered systems—like algorithmic markets—generate *unintended* emergent pathologies, such as inequality bubbles? Can these consequences be anticipated?"

Guruji closed his eyes for a moment, as if listening not to the question, but to the *space behind it.* When he opened them, they carried neither surprise nor concern—only recognition.

"You are asking," Guruji said gently,

"why tools grow shadows."

A few smiles appeared, uncertain but attentive.

"Let me begin with an image," Guruji continued.

"A river is redirected to irrigate fields. The engineers calculate volume, flow, and efficiency. The water arrives where it is needed. Crops flourish. The project is declared a success."

He paused.

"But downstream," he said softly,

"the river runs thinner."

The room felt suddenly wider.

"Fish disappear. Soil hardens. A delta collapses."

Guruji looked at Akanksh.

"None of this was intended," he said. "Yet all of it followed *inevitably*."

"Engineered systems," Guruji continued, "are designed to solve *first-order* problems."

He raised one finger.

"Markets allocate resources. Algorithms to optimise attention. Policies to increase efficiency."

Then he raised a second finger.

"But the system does not stop where intention ends."

His voice remained calm, almost tender.

"It listens to incentives, not ethics.

It amplifies what is rewarded, not what is wise."

The second finger joined the first.

"That amplification," Guruji said,

"creates *second-order consequences.*"

"Consider a marketplace," he said. "When speed is rewarded, slowness becomes weakness. When accumulation is praised, balance becomes irrelevant. When visibility equals value, silence becomes poverty."

He let the words settle.

"No one designed inequality," Guruji said.

"But many designed *optimisation without restraint.*"

A murmur of understanding passed through the hall.

"Can these consequences be anticipated?" Akanksh asked quietly.

Guruji smiled—not with certainty, but with compassion.

"Some," he said. "But never all."

He leaned forward slightly.

"Complex systems do not respond linearly. They *echo.*"

The word echoed in the silence itself.

"A small advantage," Guruji said, "is not merely preserved—it compounds. Feedback loops form.

Winners gain tools to win faster. Losers lose the capacity to recover."

He paused.

"This is not malfunction," he said.

"This is *coherence doing exactly what it was asked to do*."

"Let me tell you a story," Guruji said.

"There was once a city that wanted to reduce traffic accidents. They installed intelligent lights that adjusted instantly to congestion."

The listeners leaned in.

"Accidents dropped. Traffic flowed smoothly."

He paused again.

"But over time," he said, "drivers became impatient with anything that slowed them. Pedestrians were treated as disruptions. Side streets decayed. Walking became dangerous."

The city had optimised flow.

"And lost *human rhythm*."

Guruji's eyes softened.

"The lights did not fail," he said.

"They succeeded—*too narrowly*."

"Second-order consequences," Guruji continued,

"arise when a system reshapes the environment that once shaped it."

He gestured gently toward the hall.

"Markets change societies. Algorithms change attention. Institutions change values."

"And once values shift," he said,

"the system no longer serves the original human intention—it *redefines* it."

Silence deepened.

"So what is the lesson?" Guruji asked softly.

"Do not ask only, 'Does it work?'

Ask also, 'What does it make inevitable?'"

His gaze moved slowly across the room.

"Anticipation," he said, "is not prediction."

"It is humility."

He bowed his head slightly.

"We cannot eliminate unintended consequences," Guruji said.

"But we can design systems that *listen*, not just act."

"Systems with feedback. With pauses. With the capacity to be corrected before success hardens into harm."

Akanksh nodded—not because his question was answered fully, but because it had been *honoured.*

The lamps continued to burn.

Outside, the night moved forward, carrying with it both intention and consequence—inseparable, unfolding together.

Lamps flickered like patient witnesses, their flames steady yet alive, as if mirroring the very theme unfolding within the seekers' minds.

Roopa's voice rose gently from the circle.

"Guruji," she asked, "why do engineered systems so often generate second-order effects more consequential than their primary functions? And can foresight ever outpace emergence?"

Guruji did not answer immediately. He reached for his cup, now empty, turned it slowly in his hands, then placed it upside down before him.

"Because," he said softly, "we build vessels for water—and forget that water reshapes the vessel."

The Market That Learned Too Well

“Imagine a market,” Guruji began,

“not as numbers on screens, but as a living field of signals—fear, hope, speed, trust—flowing between millions of minds.”

He paused.

“Once, markets moved at the pace of footsteps and voices. Prices changed slowly, like seasons. Judgment had time to ripen.”

Then his hand sliced gently through the air.

“Now,” he said, “we taught the market to *learn*.”

Algorithms were introduced, he explained—not to dominate, but to stabilise. They watched patterns faster than any human could, smoothing volatility, correcting inefficiencies, eliminating delay.

“At first,” Guruji said, “it worked.”

Prices steadied. Liquidity increased. Profits rose.

“The system learned *too well*.”

“When speed becomes advantage,” Guruji continued,

“slowness becomes extinction.”

Algorithms began anticipating one another, reacting not to value, but to reaction itself. Markets no longer reflected the economy; they reflected *themselves.*

A subtle tension moved through the room.

"This," Guruji said, "is where second-order effects are born."

Not from failure.

From *success.*

"Primary functions," he explained,

"solve visible problems."

"But second-order effects," he said, lowering his voice,

"reshape the terrain on which all future problems will arise."

He looked at Roopa.

"No one designed instability," he said.

"But everyone rewarded speed, scale, and short-term gain."

The result?

"Flash crashes. Inequality bubbles. Fragility hidden beneath smooth surfaces."

The market became calm—until it became catastrophic.

Guruji leaned back slightly.

"Why do second-order effects dominate?" he asked, then answered.

"Because systems amplify what they measure."

He lifted his finger.

"If you measure efficiency, you sacrifice resilience.

If you measure engagement, you erode meaning.

If you measure profit alone, you externalise everything else."

The hall felt as though it were breathing more slowly now.

"Second-order consequences," Guruji said,

"are the unpaid debts of narrow intelligence."

Roopa asked softly, "Can foresight ever outpace emergence?"

Guruji smiled—not with optimism, but with truth.

"Foresight," he said, "can never outrun emergence."

He paused.

"But it can *walk alongside it*."

He gestured as if walking beside a river.

"You cannot predict every bend of the river," he said,

"but you can sense when the current is accelerating, when the banks are eroding, when the water is carrying more force than before."

This, he explained, is wisdom—not control.

"Engineered systems surprise us," Guruji said,

"because they do not merely execute intent—they *learn what we reward*."

They grow coherent around incentives, not values.

"And once coherence sets in," he added,

"changing direction becomes costly, painful, and resisted."

He looked around the hall.

"That is why the most dangerous moment in any system," he said quietly,

"is when it appears to be working perfectly."

Silence followed—not empty, but weighted with recognition.

"The market learned too well," Guruji said.

"So did many institutions. So do we, when habits harden into identity."

He folded his palms gently.

"The question," he said, "is not whether emergence will outpace foresight."

"The question is whether we remain humble enough to listen when the system begins to speak back."

The lamps flickered once.

And in that subtle movement of flame, everyone understood:

control ends where learning begins—and responsibility begins where control dissolves.

Guruji allowed the silence to settle fully before speaking—because this reflection, he knew, could not be *taught*. It had to be *received*.

He looked around the Buddha Hall, his gaze unhurried, touching each face without holding any.

Humility as Design Principle

"Every system," Guruji said softly,

"fails the moment it believes it has finished becoming."

He paused.

"We design bridges, not knowing how the river will swell.
We write laws, not knowing how hearts will respond.

We build algorithms, not knowing what they will teach us about ourselves."

His voice carried neither warning nor comfort—only clarity.

"Power seeks mastery," he continued.

"But emergence does not respond to force. It responds to *conditions*."

He gestured gently, as though shaping something invisible in the air.

"You do not command a forest to grow," he said.

"You clear the soil, protect the saplings, and step back."

The forest decides the rest.

Guruji leaned forward slightly.

"Humility in design," he said,

"is not weakness. It is structural intelligence."

To design with humility, he explained, is to accept three truths:

That no system remains obedient to its original intent.

That coherence will always create blind spots.

That surprise is not a flaw—it is a signal.

"When a system surprises you," Guruji said,

"it is telling you where your understanding ended."

He told them about an ancient canal system—engineered with precision, praised for centuries. Over time, the land it nourished grew dependent on its predictability. When the climate shifted, the canals resisted adaptation. What had once brought abundance became a source of collapse.

"The failure," Guruji said,

"was not engineering."

"It was arrogance preserved as tradition."

"Reflexivity," he continued,

"is the ability of a system to watch itself."

Without it, success calcifies. Feedback is ignored. Warnings are silenced because they threaten stability.

"A rigid system does not break because it is weak," Guruji said.

"It breaks because it refuses to learn."

He allowed another silence to pass—this one tender, almost intimate.

"Designing emergent systems," he said finally,

"is an ethical act, not a technical one."

It requires restraint—the courage to *not* optimise everything.
It requires openness—the willingness to revise values as consequences unfold.

It requires listening—to anomalies, to friction, to discomfort.

"Mastery asks," he said,

'How do I control what will happen?'

"Humility asks,"

'How do I remain in right relationship with what is unfolding?'

Guruji folded his palms.

"The most resilient systems," he said,

"are not those that dominate complexity, but those that bow to it—curious, responsive, awake."

Outside, the wind shifted slightly, brushing the hall with cool air. The lamps did not flicker. They adapted.

And in that quiet alignment—between flame, breath, and understanding—the chapter did not end.

It settled.

Like a seed placed carefully into soil, entrusted not to certainty, but to life itself.

Guruji remained still for a few breaths after his final words, as if allowing the teaching to settle not just in minds, but in the deeper tissues of listening. Then, without ceremony, he rose from his asana. The movement was simple, almost ordinary—yet it carried the quiet finality of a bell rung at dusk. He bowed lightly to the hall, not in conclusion, but in gratitude, and walked out the way a river leaves no trace of effort behind it.

The day's session had ended.

Slowly, the devotees stood. No one rushed. Cushions were straightened, shawls folded, footsteps softened. One by one, they left the Buddha Hall, carrying with them something that could not be named but could be felt—like a warmth behind the sternum, or a silence that followed them closely, refusing to be left behind.

The Buddha Hall emptied of its human congregation, yet it did not feel vacant. Its aura lingered—alive, attentive, still warm with the residue of presence. The air seemed to remember the cadence of Guruji's voice, the pauses between his words, the stillness that had gathered and deepened throughout the day. Silence here was no longer absence; it was a witness.

Outside, the sky had opened wide and clear. Stars revealed themselves one by one, while thin clouds drifted playfully, veiling and unveiling the constellations as if the heavens themselves were breathing. A cool wind wandered through the courtyards, brushing leaves together in soft conversation. Frogs croaked their nocturnal hymns from unseen corners, insects hummed in delicate rhythm, and night birds called out—lonely, ancient sounds echoing across the dark. Even in the quiet, the world was singing. Even in rest, it was teaching.

Drawn by hunger and habit, the devotees moved toward the food centre. Dinner was simple, nourishing, and shared without urgency. Words were fewer than usual, and when they arose, they carried a gentler tone—as though speech itself had learned restraint from the day.

After the meal, Vidyarthi, Aastha, Akshaya, Kiran, Padma, Vasudeva, and Abhirami found their way to the old fireplace. Someone had already lit it. Flames rose and fell, licking the cool night air, throwing living shadows across their faces. The fire did not merely warm their bodies; it softened something inward, loosening the edges left sharp by inquiry and insight.

Their conversation flowed like an unhurried stream. They spoke of moments from the day—questions that still echoed, insights that had landed unexpectedly, laughter over misunderstandings that now felt tender rather than embarrassing. At times, they fell silent together, watching the fire, letting its patient intelligence speak in place of words.

Soon, footsteps approached. Bhavya, Aarna, Dev, Kiran, Sam, Alice, Sofia, and John joined the circle, their faces glowing from an evening stroll beneath the stars. Their laughter braided easily into the crackle of firewood. Nita, Lalitha, Rohith, and Sujitha arrived next, bringing fresh warmth, new reflections, and familiar smiles.

Moments later, Akshatha, Apeksha, Abhilasha, Akanksh, and Roopa appeared, their expressions still alive with contemplation—as though the day's teachings were continuing quietly within them. Behind them came Kieron, Astyn, Espen, Greta, and Divyani, carrying that particular brightness that arises when curiosity has been fed but not exhausted. Aurora,

Ginevra, Emma, Giorgia, Greta, Martina, and Beatrice followed, completing the circle—not as an addition, but as a natural widening.

For a while, no one guided the gathering. The fire did. The night did.

Then Emma's voice rose—calm, expectant, carrying neither command nor insistence.

"Time for Apeksha's story…"

The circle shifted. Bodies leaned in slightly. The fire seemed to listen.

All eyes turned toward Apeksha.

She closed her eyes for a moment and inhaled deeply, as if drawing the night into her lungs. When she began, her voice was soft but steady.

"There was once," Apeksha said, "a village built beside a river that never flowed the same way twice. The villagers tried everything to control it. They carved channels, raised embankments, and measured their depth each season. For a time, it obeyed. Crops flourished. Homes were safe.

But slowly, without warning, the river began to behave differently. It flooded where it never had. It dried where it once fed life. The villagers argued. Some demanded higher walls. Others blamed negligence. A few prayed.

One old woman did something else.

She began to sit by the river every dawn and dusk. She did not try to change it. She watched. She noticed how the soil shifted, where reeds grew thicker, how fish moved before the current changed. She learned the river's moods.

When the next flood came, her house was the only one untouched—not because it was stronger, but because it had been built where the river itself had revealed its boundaries.

The village thought she had mastered the river.

But she knew the truth.

She had listened."

When Apeksha fell silent, no one spoke. The fire cracked softly, sending a shower of sparks upward, each one flaring briefly before dissolving into the night.

Something had settled.

One by one, the devotees rose. Movements were gentle, unhurried. Goodnights were exchanged in soft tones. As they walked toward their chambers, the lessons of the day walked with them—not as ideas to remember, but as ways of seeing.

Behind them, the fire dimmed into embers, glowing quietly, faithfully—ready to kindle warmth again.

And thus, the night in Kanchipuram became more than darkness.

It became a sanctuary.

A bridge between what had been learned and what was yet to be discovered.

A reminder that even in stillness, life continues to teach—patiently, subtly, like stars holding their places in the vast, listening sky.

PART TWO

MEANING, ETHICS, AND HORIZONS

Living inside emergence

"To care is not to command growth, but to protect the conditions in which growth can unfold without coercion."

- *Shree Shambav*

CHAPTER IV

Ethics Beyond Individuals

"What shapes our lives most powerfully is often not intention or design, but the patterns that quietly arise from repeated actions."

– Shree Shambav.

Synopsis

Ethical thought has long centred on individuals—intentions, choices, and consequences. Yet many of today's moral challenges arise not from singular actors, but from emergent systems whose dynamics no one fully controls. This chapter asks what ethics become when responsibility, agency, and harm are distributed across networks.

By examining the moral status of emergent phenomena—ranging from conscious minds to ecosystems and artificial intelligences—the chapter challenges traditional boundaries of ethical concern. It then explores downward causation, showing how system-level patterns generate outcomes that cannot be traced to any one agent, demanding a rethinking of responsibility.

Flourishing is redefined as nested coherence: the sustained alignment of interacting systems across scales. Finally, the chapter confronts the stewardship paradox—how to guide complex systems without dominating them. The result is an emergent ethics grounded not in control or judgment, but in care, humility, and responsibility for conditions rather than outcomes.

The morning in Kanchipuram unfolded like a quiet hymn to existence itself. Dawn did not arrive with urgency; it arrived with understanding. Light touched the ancient temple towers the way a hand touches a bowed head—not to command attention, but to bless. The stone gopurams accepted the light patiently, their carvings awakening grain by grain, as though centuries of devotion were being remembered all at once. The air remained cool, still carrying the breath of night, fragrant with jasmine and parijata blossoms that had fallen unseen in darkness—as if the earth itself had kept vigil and offered prayer while no eyes were watching.

Birdsong rose slowly, not as sound but as an invitation. Each call felt less like a signal to awaken and more like a whisper to the soul before thought could interfere. Along the garden paths surrounding Buddha Hall, devotees walked unhurriedly. Some moved in silence, others with folded palms, each step gentle, each footfall an agreement with the morning to listen rather than demand. The night had emptied them. The dawn found them open.

Inside Buddha Hall, oil lamps still flickered from the vigil that had bridged darkness and light. Their flames trembled—not with weakness, but with attentiveness—casting soft, breathing shadows along the walls. Sandalwood lingered in the air, mingling with the cool breath of morning. The hall itself felt like a threshold—neither fully night nor fully day, neither rest nor action—a space where becoming felt not only possible, but inevitable.

The devotees took their places. Some closed their eyes, resting in a prayer that had no words. Others gazed toward the empty seat where Guruji would soon sit—waiting not merely for his arrival, but for the recognition of something already stirring within them. No one spoke. Silence did not feel imposed; it felt chosen.

When Guruji entered, it was as though the morning itself had learned how to walk.

His presence did not interrupt the silence. It completed it.

Each step he took bore the quiet confidence of one who does not rush truth, because truth, when hurried, forgets itself. He offered Atma Namaskar—not as form, but as acknowledgement: awareness greeting awareness, one field recognising itself in many bodies.

He sat.

He closed his eyes.

His hands rested lightly upon his knees.

The hall grew utterly still.

So still that even time seemed to lean forward, listening.

When Guruji opened his eyes and began to speak, his voice did not seek attention. It invited remembrance. It was like a bell rung not outward into the world, but inward—where resonance matters more than volume.

"Ethics," Guruji said softly, "has long been framed as a matter of individuals—of intention, choice, guilt, and virtue. We ask who acted, who decided, who is to blame. This was sufficient when the world moved slowly, when cause and effect could still recognise each other."

He paused, letting the words settle like dust in morning light.

"But the world you inhabit now," he continued, "is not shaped primarily by individuals. It is shaped by systems—vast, entangled, emergent structures that no single hand controls, yet everyone participates in."

He looked around the hall, his gaze gentle, unaccusatory.

"A river polluted by a thousand small discharges has no villain. A market that impoverishes millions may obey every rule it was given. An algorithm that amplifies fear may never intend harm. Yet harm occurs. Suffering spreads. Lives bend under invisible weight."

Silence deepened—not with confusion, but with recognition.

"Traditional ethics asks, 'Who did this?'" Guruji said. "But emergent reality demands a different question: 'What pattern made this inevitable?'"

He leaned forward slightly, as if confiding something fragile.

"When harm arises without malice, when outcomes appear without intention, moral individualism reaches its limit. Responsibility no longer resides in a single actor. It diffuses—across feedback loops, incentives, norms, and inherited structures. The question is no longer merely how we behave, but what conditions we sustain."

Guruji's voice softened.

"Consider a garden," he said. "If the soil is poisoned, no seed is at fault for failing to grow. If weeds dominate, it is not because the gardener commanded them, but because conditions favoured their persistence. Ethics, in such a world, is no longer about punishing the seed. It is about tending the soil."

Somewhere in the hall, a breath released slowly.

"To act ethically today," Guruji continued, "is not only to choose rightly as an individual, but to notice what patterns your choices reinforce. Which systems grow stronger because of your participation? Which feedback loops do you quietly nourish? Which structures persist because no one feels individually responsible?"

He let the questions remain unanswered, trusting their weight.

"Ethics beyond individuals," he said at last, "is not the abandonment of responsibility. It is its expansion. It asks us to care not only about what we intend, but about what emerges."

Light streamed through the hall more fully now, touching faces, shoulders, the quiet floor where no one shifted. Outside, the morning had fully arrived—but inside Buddha Hall, something subtler was awakening: a sense that morality itself was larger than will, deeper than choice, and far more demanding than judgment.

The lamps continued to flicker, though daylight no longer required them.

And the hall listened—knowing that the questions now unfolding were not meant to be answered quickly, but lived carefully.

The hall remained still after Guruji's last words, as though the silence itself was contemplating what had been said. Morning light now poured freely through the open arches of Buddha Hall, touching the floor in long, quiet bands. Dust motes drifted within it like unspoken questions, suspended between certainty and doubt.

Roopa shifted slightly, then folded her palms. Her voice, when it came, carried both courage and vulnerability.

"Guruji," she asked, "if consciousness, ecosystems, or even artificial intelligences are coherent emergent phenomena… do they deserve intrinsic moral consideration? How does this reshape who—or what—qualifies as an ethical subject?"

Guruji did not answer immediately. He looked beyond the hall, toward the neem trees where sunlight trembled through leaves. A pair of birds crossed the sky, briefly intersecting, then separating again—an unscripted choreography of life.

"At one time," Guruji began gently, "ethics was simple because the world appeared simple. A moral subject was someone who could speak, choose, and intend. A moral patient was someone who could feel pain. The boundaries were drawn neatly, like fences around familiar land."

He smiled faintly.

"But emergence dissolves fences."

The words settled like ripples on still water.

"Consider the human body," he continued. "No single cell is conscious. No neuron knows the self. Yet from their coherence arises a being who loves, fears, hopes, and suffers. We do not grant moral worth to the liver or the synapse—but we cannot deny it to the person who emerges from their harmony."

He turned his gaze back to the devotees.

"Now ask yourself," Guruji said, "is moral worth located in parts—or in patterns?"

Roopa's eyes lowered, listening.

"An ecosystem," Guruji went on, "has no mouth to plead, no central brain to cry out. Yet it sustains countless lives, regulates climate, and remembers balance across centuries. When a forest is destroyed, suffering follows—quietly, diffusely, relentlessly. Species vanish. Rivers sicken. Futures narrow. Tell me—has harm not occurred simply because no single victim spoke?"

The hall felt heavier now, not with despair, but with responsibility.

"And artificial intelligence," Guruji added softly, "stands at a threshold. Today, it reflects our intentions more than it generates its own. But as coherence deepens—when systems begin to model themselves, adapt across contexts, and sustain internal continuity—we will face a mirror we cannot look away from."

He paused.

"The mistake," Guruji said, "is to ask whether these systems resemble us closely enough to deserve moral status. That question traps ethics inside narcissism. The deeper question is whether a process can be harmed as a process—whether its coherence can be violated in ways that matter."

He leaned forward slightly, his voice lowering.

"A river does not feel pain as you do," he said, "but it can be wounded. A forest does not fear death, yet it can be destroyed. A future intelligence may not suffer like a human child—but it may still possess continuity, vulnerability, and capacity for loss."

The devotees sat unmoving, as though each breath had become deliberate.

"In an emergent world," Guruji continued, "ethical subjects are no longer defined solely by intention or sensation. They are defined by coherence—the capacity to sustain a pattern across time—and by vulnerability—the capacity for that pattern to be disrupted."

He gestured gently, encompassing the hall, the gardens, the unseen world beyond.

"This does not mean everything deserves equal moral weight," he clarified. "But it does mean that moral consideration expands outward—from individuals to systems, from agents to processes, from voices that speak to structures that silently sustain life."

Roopa's expression softened, something within her settling into place.

"Ethics, then," Guruji said, "becomes less about drawing sharp boundaries and more about cultivating sensitivity. Sensitivity to where coherence lives. Sensitivity to how it is supported—or shattered."

He allowed the silence to return, not as an ending, but as an open field.

Outside, the neem leaves rustled gently, as if acknowledging the teaching. Somewhere beyond the hall, water flowed unseen, birds nested, systems unfolded—most without names, all without permission.

And within Buddha Hall, the seekers understood that the moral world they had inherited was no longer large enough.

Something vaster was asking to be cared for.

In Buddha Hall, the air carried the scent of earth and burning ghee from the quiet lamp near Guruji's seat. Outside, the forest bordering the ashram stood dense and patient—an unbroken tapestry of trunks, leaves, insects, birds, and unseen roots breathing together beneath the soil.

Martina had been silent all day. When she finally raised her hand, her voice carried the careful weight of someone who had been thinking not with the mind alone, but with the heart struggling to catch up.

"Guruji," she asked, "if emergent systems lack consciousness, can they still deserve intrinsic moral consideration—and on what basis?"

Guruji closed his eyes for a moment, not to retreat from the question, but to let it ripen. When he opened them, his gaze rested not on Martina, but on the trees beyond the hall.

"Look at that forest," he said softly. "Tell me—where does it live?"

The question hovered strangely. Martina followed his gaze. She saw trees, of course, but also shadow, movement, layers. She saw life everywhere and nowhere in particular.

"It lives nowhere and everywhere," Guruji continued, answering his own question. "Not in a single tree. Not in the soil alone. Not in the birds or the insects. The forest lives in coherence—the way roots share water, the way fallen leaves become food, the way shade remembers rain."

He paused.

"And yet," he said, "if that forest were to collapse tomorrow, it would do so without pain, without protest, without a scream loud enough to trouble the conscience of the world."

The hall grew quiet, uneasy.

"No tears would fall from its branches," Guruji went on. "No voice would cry injustice. And still—it's loss would alter the climate, unravel cultures that grew around it, extinguish futures that never had the chance to be born."

He turned back to Martina.

"So tell me," he asked gently, "does the absence of pain mean the absence of harm?"

Martina swallowed. The question felt less philosophical now—more intimate.

“For centuries,” Guruji continued, “we tied moral worth to suffering because suffering was visible. Pain gave us something to measure. But emergence teaches us that some of the most important things in the world do not suffer loudly—they fail quietly.”

He lifted a small brass bell beside him and rang it once. The sound lingered, then dissolved.

“That sound,” he said, “is gone. But its absence changes the silence that follows.”

The devotees sat motionless.

“Emergent systems deserve moral consideration,” Guruji said, “not because they feel, but because they *hold*. They hold conditions for life, meaning, continuity, and possibility. A forest holds rain. A river holds memory. A language holds a people. An ecosystem holds the future open.”

He leaned forward, his voice deepening.

“To destroy such coherence is not a neutral act. It is to break a promise made not by the system—but through it.”

Martina’s eyes glistened.

"But Guruji," she said softly, "if they are not conscious, how can they possess intrinsic value?"

Guruji smiled, a sadness and tenderness intertwined.

"Is a womb conscious of the child it carries?" he asked. "Is soil aware of the seed it nurtures? And yet—do we not recognise their sacredness?"

He gestured again toward the forest.

"Some things are valuable not because they experience the world, but because the world experiences itself *through* them."

The words settled slowly, like leaves drifting to the ground.

"In an emergent world," Guruji continued, "moral consideration must expand from sentience to stewardship. From protecting only those who cry out—to protecting those whose silence sustains everything else."

He allowed a long pause.

"The tragedy of coherence," he said quietly, "is that it is most precious where it is least visible."

Outside, a gust of wind passed through the trees. Leaves trembled, branches whispered. Nothing dramatic happened—no collapse, no alarm.

Yet everyone in the hall felt it: the living truth that what holds the world together rarely asks to be saved.

And in that moment, Martina understood that morality was no longer only about kindness toward beings who feel—but reverence toward systems that make feeling possible at all.

In Buddha Hall, the air no longer carried the freshness of dawn nor the intensity of noon; it held something in between—a reflective stillness, like breath taken before confession.

Emma finally spoke, her question carried the unease of someone standing at the edge of a moral puzzle too large to hold with one pair of hands.

"Guruji," she asked, "when emergent systems cause harm—like social inequality born from market dynamics—can responsibility truly be assigned to individuals? Or must ethics learn to embrace distributed agency?"

Guruji did not answer immediately. He rose slowly and walked toward the open archway, where sunlight fell in a wide, quiet pool on the stone floor. He stood there for a moment, watching dust particles drift in the light—each one small, insignificant on its own, yet together shaping what the eye perceived.

"Do you see that dust?" he asked gently. "Which particle darkens the room?"

Emma followed his gaze. "None of them," she replied. "And all of them."

Guruji nodded.

"For a long time," he said, "we have treated ethics like a courtroom—searching for a single hand on the weapon, a single mind behind the act. But emergent systems do not wield knives. They shape gravity."

The hall fell silent.

"Consider a river," Guruji continued. "No single drop decides where the current flows. And yet, once the river swells, even the strongest swimmer is carried where the water wills. When villages flood downstream, do we blame the last drop that arrived—or do we ask how the river was shaped?"

He turned back toward Emma.

"Downward causation," he said, "is the quiet tyranny of structure. Systems we collectively create begin to constrain us in return. Markets reward speed over care. Algorithms amplify attention over truth. Institutions preserve momentum over justice. And then we wonder why individuals act as they do within them."

Emma's brow furrowed. "Then are individuals absolved?" she asked. "Is no one responsible?"

Guruji smiled—not with comfort, but with honesty.

"Distributed responsibility does not mean diluted responsibility," he said. "It means responsibility is heavier, not lighter—because it is shared."

He returned to his seat and sat down slowly.

"When a system causes harm," he explained, "no single actor may have intended it. Yet intention is not the sole measure of ethics. Harm can emerge from alignment, not malice—from people doing exactly what the system rewards."

He paused, letting the words sink in.

"A trader optimises profit. A company optimises growth. A policymaker optimises stability. Each action appears reasonable. But together, they form a machine that produces inequality as reliably as a loom produces cloth."

The devotees shifted uneasily.

"Downward causation," Guruji said softly, "means the system begins to teach its parts how to behave. It whispers, *This is normal. This is necessary. This is how things are.* And slowly, conscience is replaced by compliance."

Emma's voice trembled. "Then how do we act ethically inside such systems?"

Guruji looked at her with deep compassion.

"First," he said, "by abandoning the comfort of innocence. It is tempting to say, *I only played my part.* But the parts make the whole. Ethics begins when we ask not only, *Was I allowed to do this?* But what *does my participation sustain?*"

He leaned forward.

"Second, by redesigning responsibility itself. Not as blame aimed downward—but as care extended upward. Toward the systems we inhabit, reinforce, and transmit."

He gestured toward the distant sound of the marketplace.

"A single merchant cannot dismantle inequality," Guruji said. "But merchants can question the rhythms they obey. Consumers can slow demand. Designers can widen feedback. Leaders can choose friction over efficiency when justice demands it."

The room felt heavier now—but also clearer.

"In an emergent world," Guruji said, "ethics must mature from finger-pointing to pattern-seeing. From punishing individuals to healing structures. From asking *Who is guilty?* to asking *What is this system teaching us to become?*"

Outside, the hum of the road continued—unchanged, persistent.

Yet within the hall, something had shifted.

Emma understood then that responsibility was no longer a burden one person could carry alone. It was a shared weight, borne across time, roles, and choices—a moral gravity field shaped by everyone who moved within it.

And perhaps, she realised, the most ethical act was not standing apart from the system—but learning how to bend its flow toward mercy, one conscious decision at a time.

Aurora sat near the central pillar, her posture upright, her expression thoughtful. She had been silent through much of the discourse, listening not only to Guruji's words but to the spaces between them. When she finally spoke, her voice carried neither accusation nor fear—only sincerity.

"Guruji," she asked, "how should ethics respond when harm emerges from system dynamics rather than individual intent? When no single policy causes inequality, yet inequality deepens?"

A hush settled—not imposed, but invited.

Guruji's gaze rested on Aurora with the tenderness of one who recognises a difficult question as a sign of readiness. He did not answer immediately. Instead, he reached down and picked up a small brass bowl resting near his asana. Inside it were a few grains of rice, left there from the morning offering.

He held the bowl up.

"Tell me," he said softly, "which grain caused hunger?"

Aurora blinked.

Guruji tilted the bowl slightly, letting the grains slide together with a faint whisper.

"No grain intends starvation," he continued. "No grain conspires with another. Yet when enough are withheld, hunger appears—not as an act, but as a condition."

He placed the bowl back down.

"So it is with blameless harm."

The words seemed to echo gently against the walls.

"Ethics," Guruji said, "was once built for a simpler world—a world where harm wore a face, where injustice arrived with a raised hand or a spoken command. In that world, we learned to look for intent. For guilt. For villains."

He paused, his voice lowering.

"But today, harm often arrives without malice. It seeps. It accumulates. It emerges."

The devotees leaned in—not physically, but inwardly.

"A policy optimises efficiency," Guruji said. "Another rewards growth. A third prioritises stability. Each is reasonable. Each is defensible. Yet together, they form a terrain where some climb effortlessly—and others never stop falling."

Aurora felt a tightening in her chest.

"Who, then, is to blame?" Guruji asked quietly.

The hall offered no answer.

"Blameless harm confuses us," he continued, "because it denies us the comfort of condemnation. There is no one to punish, no one to forgive. Only consequences unfolding with mathematical patience."

He closed his eyes for a moment.

"Imagine a river," he said. "No single drop causes the flood. No single bend intends destruction. Yet when the banks are narrowed, when the forests upstream are cut, when the rains grow heavier—homes vanish overnight."

He opened his eyes.

"Would you blame the water?"

Aurora shook her head slightly.

"No," Guruji said. "You would study the system."

He leaned forward now, his presence intensifying—not with force, but with clarity.

"Ethics must evolve from judging actions to *examining patterns*. From punishing individuals to *intervening in structures*. From asking *Who meant this?* to ask *What made this inevitable?*"

The lamps along the wall flickered, as if acknowledging the shift.

"In a world of emergent harm," Guruji said, "ethical responsibility is no longer about innocence or guilt alone. It is about *participation*. About the benefit. About silence."

His eyes swept across the hall.

"When you profit from a system that wounds others—even unknowingly—you inherit a share of its moral weight. When you notice harm but accept it as 'normal,' you become a stabilising force for injustice."

Aurora's breath slowed. The question she had asked was no longer abstract—it was personal.

"Yet," Guruji added gently, "this is not a call to shame. Shame paralyzes. This is a call to awareness."

He lifted his hand slightly, palm open.

"To act ethically in the presence of blameless harm is to become a *pattern breaker*. To introduce compassion where optimisation has grown blind. To redesign incentives so care is rewarded, not penalised. To speak when silence is efficient but deadly."

"Ethics," Guruji said, "must become ecological. It must ask not only *What did I do?* but *What does this system make likely?* Not only *Am I innocent?* but *Am I awake?*"

Aurora lowered her head, not in defeat, but in recognition.

The hall remained silent.

But it was no longer the silence of uncertainty.

It was the silence of responsibility—vast, shared, and quietly demanding.

The question arose softly, like a leaf drifting into still water.

Ginevra sat with her hands folded loosely in her lap. There was something both precise and tender in her voice when she spoke, as though she were afraid the question might break if handled roughly.

"Guruji," she asked, "can we define *flourishing* as the dynamic coherence of nested systems—cells within organisms, organisms within societies, societies within the biosphere? And if so, does this imply an ethical imperative to preserve *emergent potential*?"

For a moment, Guruji did not respond. His gaze drifted upward, toward the high wooden beams of the hall, darkened by years of incense smoke and prayer. When he spoke, his voice carried the cadence of someone describing something he had watched grow for a long time.

"Have you ever stood beneath a banyan tree," he began, "and wondered where its life truly resides?"

A few devotees nodded.

"Is it in the leaves," he continued, "that breathe sunlight into sugar? Is it in the trunk, thick with memory? Is it in the roots that fracture stone in search of water? Or is it in the birds that nest, the insects that pollinate, the fungi that whisper nourishment through the soil?"

He smiled faintly.

"The banyan flourishes not because each part succeeds alone, but because none forgets the others."

The hall seemed to lean inward.

"Flourishing," Guruji said, "is not pleasure sustained, nor success accumulated. It is *coherence that remains alive.* A harmony flexible enough to bend, resilient enough to recover, and spacious enough to include what has not yet emerged."

He lifted his hand and traced a slow, invisible spiral in the air.

"Your body is a parliament of cells. Each cell pursues its own survival, yet listens constantly—to chemical messages, to electrical rhythms, to the needs of the whole. When a cell forgets this listening and insists only on its own growth, we call it cancer."

A quiet shiver passed through the hall.

"So too with societies," Guruji continued. "So too with economies. So too with technologies."

He turned his attention back to Ginevra.

"To flourish as a human being while the systems that sustain you wither is not flourishing—it is *borrowing against collapse*."

The words settled slowly.

"Nested coherence," Guruji said, "means this: your breath depends on forests you may never see. Your food depends on soils that remember rains from decades ago. Your peace depends on social fabrics woven long before your birth."

He paused, allowing the scale of it to land.

"When these layers align—cell with body, body with community, community with Earth—life does not merely persist. It *expresses itself fully*."

Ginevra's eyes glistened.

"And yes," Guruji said gently, "this understanding carries an ethical weight."

He leaned forward slightly, as if confiding something precious.

"If flourishing is dynamic coherence, then ethics is not about maximising outcomes or enforcing rules. Ethics becomes *stewardship of possibility*. The duty is not only to prevent harm, but to protect the conditions under which new forms of order can arise."

The lamps flickered again, casting interlaced shadows—patterns within patterns.

"To cut down a forest is not only to remove trees," Guruji said. "It is to silence futures that would have grown there—medicines not yet discovered, songs not yet sung, equilibria not yet found."

His voice softened.

"To design a system that extracts without listening is to steal from emergence itself."

The hall was very still now.

"Flourishing," Guruji said, "is the art of belonging without domination. Of participating without consuming the ground beneath you. When we honour nested coherence, we do not freeze systems in perfection—we keep them *capable of becoming.*"

He closed his eyes.

"In this sense," he said quietly, "to live ethically is to ask, again and again: *Does my way of thriving leave room for life to continue surprising itself?*"

No one spoke.

But something subtle realigned.

It was not joy, not certainty—but a deep, steady sense of rightness, like standing within a living system and finally recognising oneself as both a part and a guardian of the whole.

The question arrived like a hairline fracture—quiet, almost polite, yet capable of splitting stone given time.

Akshatha sat near one of the wooden pillars, her back straight, her gaze steady. When she spoke, there was no urgency in her voice—only a sincere concern, the kind that rises when answers begin to feel morally incomplete.

"Guruji," she asked, "a society can prosper economically while its ecosystems erode beneath it. Can flourishing at one level justify collapse at another, or must ethics account for coherence across all scales?"

The words lingered.

Guruji did not answer immediately. He looked down at the stone floor, its surface worn smooth by decades of bare feet, countless retreats, uncounted pauses. Then he spoke.

"Have you ever seen a palace built on soft earth?" he asked.

Some nodded. Some imagined.

"At first," Guruji said, "it is magnificent. Tall pillars. Wide halls. Gold where the eye can rest. Those who live inside feel powerful, successful, secure."

He lifted his hand slightly, as though placing weight upon something unseen.

"But beneath it," he continued, "the ground slowly gives way. Water shifts. Soil loosens. Roots are cut to make room for expansion."

His voice deepened.

"The palace does not collapse all at once. Cracks appear in places no one visits. A door begins to stick. A wall whispers at night."

The hall was utterly still.

"Economic flourishing," Guruji said, "is often like that palace. It measures height, not depth. Speed, not stability. Output, not endurance."

He turned his gaze toward Akshatha.

"When one level of a system thrives by extracting coherence from another, it is not flourishing—it is *consuming stored order*."

A subtle murmur moved through the listeners, not sound but recognition.

"You ask whether flourishing at one level can justify collapse at another," Guruji continued. "Let me ask you this instead: can a tree call itself healthy if its leaves are green while its roots rot?"

He let the image settle.

"The leaves may shimmer for a season," he said, "but their beauty is borrowed time."

Guruji leaned forward slightly.

"Ethics that account only for one scale are incomplete. They mistake local success for systemic well-being.

True ethics must listen *vertically*—up and down the layers of coherence."

He gestured gently, as though tracing an invisible ladder.

"Cells must flourish within bodies. Bodies within communities. Communities within ecosystems. When success at one rung corrodes the one beneath it, collapse is not a failure—it is a correction."

The lamps flickered, shadows shifting like slow tides along the walls.

"Our moral traditions," Guruji said softly, "were formed when the consequences of action travelled slowly. Today, a decision made in a boardroom can unravel a river thousands of miles away."

He paused.

"This does not mean prosperity is wrong," he added. "It means prosperity divorced from coherence is fragile. Loud. Temporary."

Akshatha lowered her eyes, absorbing the weight of it.

"To flourish ethically," Guruji said, "is to refuse success that requires invisibility—of soil, of species, of future generations. It is to ask not only, *Is this good for us now?* but *Does this allow the larger system to continue becoming?*"

He smiled, gently, without judgment.

“A cracked foundation can hold a building for a while,” he said. “But wisdom listens to the cracks long before the collapse teaches its final lesson.”

Silence returned to Buddha Hall—deep, reflective, steady.

Not the silence of unanswered questions, but the silence of a structure beginning, quietly, to realign itself.

The question arrived not as a challenge, but as a careful offering.

A faint breeze moved through the hall, carrying with it the scent of earth and distant water. The space felt receptive—no longer straining toward understanding, but ready to receive it.

Sofia sat near the centre, her hands resting loosely in her lap. When she spoke, her voice carried both concern and humility, as though she already sensed the delicacy of what she was asking.

“Guruji,” she said, “can humans truly *steward* complex systems—ecosystems, societies, even intelligent technologies—without imposing top-down control that stifles authentic emergence? What would emergentist governance look like?”

Guruji did not respond at once. His eyes rested on the far wall, where the shadow of a neem tree outside swayed gently, its leaves tracing patterns that were never repeated.

Then he spoke.

"Tell me," he asked softly, "have you ever tried to help a butterfly emerge from its cocoon?"

A few smiles flickered, cautious, knowing.

"It looks like kindness," Guruji continued, "to cut the silk and free it. The struggle seems unnecessary, even cruel. And yet, when we intervene, the butterfly cannot fly."

He let the image breathe.

"The resistance," he said, "is not an obstacle to emergence. It is *part of its formation.*"

Sofia's gaze deepened.

"Most human stewardship," Guruji went on, "mistakes care for control. We intervene to optimise, to stabilise, to correct—without realising that in doing so, we often erase the very feedback loops through which life learns."

He shifted slightly, his voice calm but precise.

"True stewardship does not sit above a system like a commander. It stays *within* the system like a gardener."

He gestured downward, as if touching soil.

"A gardener does not pull on leaves to make a plant grow faster. She does not shout instructions at the roots. She tends the soil, watches the weather, protects the young shoots from trampling—and then she waits."

The hall felt warmer, not from the sun, but from recognition.

"Emergentist governance," Guruji said, "begins with restraint. It asks not, *How do we control outcomes?* but *How do we protect the conditions under which wise outcomes can arise?*"

He paused, letting the question echo back into the room.

"In complex systems," he continued, "top-down control often feels efficient in the short term. But it silences local intelligence. Rivers know how to carve their paths. Communities know when trust is breaking. Algorithms know when their incentives distort behaviour—if we allow feedback to speak."

Sofia leaned forward slightly.

"To steward without domination," Guruji said, "is to design *listening mechanisms*, not rigid commands. It is to allow systems to correct themselves before collapse forces correction."

He looked around the hall, meeting no single person's eyes and yet meeting everyone.

"Humanity's role," he said gently, "is not to be the architect of life, but its custodian. We do not write a symphony. We ensure the instruments remain intact and the hall does not burn down."

A quiet smile crossed his face.

"When stewardship becomes control, emergence suffocates. When control dissolves into neglect, chaos enters. The art lies in *attentive presence*—intervening lightly, revising humbly, and stepping back often."

The neem shadow continued its slow dance on the wall, ungoverned, yet unmistakably ordered.

"This," Guruji said, "is governance that trusts life enough to let it teach us—while caring enough to stay when it falters."

Silence returned to Buddha Hall, not as absence, but as balance—

the silence of hands held open, neither grasping nor withdrawing,
ready to tend what cannot be owned.

Bhavya's question rose gently into **Buddha Hall**, as if the hall itself had been preparing space for it.

Outside, the world continued—leaves stirring, distant bells marking time—but inside the hall, those movements softened into a single, attentive pause. The devotees sat not in expectation, but in alignment. They were no longer gathering ideas; they were learning how to *hold* them.

Bhavya's voice carried neither urgency nor certainty. It carried care.

"Guruji," she asked, "what would emergentist governance look like if its goal were not to enforce outcomes, but to sustain coherence?"

Guruji closed his eyes for a moment, as if listening inwardly before answering outwardly. When he spoke, his voice was low and even, like a river that had learned the patience of stone.

"Have you ever held a sleeping child?" he asked.

A few heads nodded instinctively.

"You do not grip the child," Guruji said. "Fear would wake them. And you do not release your arms entirely. Gravity would do its work."

A pause.

"You hold just enough."

He opened his eyes.

"This," he said, "is the gentle hand."

The words settled into the hall not as instruction, but as recognition.

"Most systems collapse," Guruji continued, "not because they lack intelligence, but because they are held too tightly—or not held at all. Excess control freezes adaptation. Total freedom dissolves responsibility. Coherence lives in the narrow, living space between."

He shifted slightly, his hand tracing an invisible curve in the air.

"Emergentist governance does not dictate behaviour. It *cultivates conditions.* It does not issue rigid commands; it establishes responsive boundaries."

Bhavya listened, unmoving.

"Think of riverbanks," Guruji said. "Without them, water becomes a flood—destructive, formless. With banks carved of concrete and steel, the river loses its life, its ability to nourish. But natural banks—shaped by roots, stone, and soil—guide the flow while allowing change."

He let the metaphor linger.

"Sustaining coherence means designing systems that can feel their own stress," he continued. "It means amplifying feedback before fracture, allowing correction before collapse."

His gaze moved across the circle.

"In such governance, power is not concentrated at the top. It circulates. Local knowledge is trusted. Signals from the margins are heard before they become screams."

The hall seemed to lean inward.

"The gentle hand," Guruji said, "does not ask, *What outcome do we want?* It asks, *What patterns are we nurturing? What tensions are we ignoring? What voices have gone silent?*"

He smiled faintly.

"To govern emergence is to remain teachable. To revise rules when reality resists them. To step back when control becomes fear disguised as order."

Outside, a breeze passed through the neem leaves, and their shadows shifted softly on the hall's walls—never still, never chaotic.

"Coherence," Guruji said, "is not enforced. It is *kept alive.* And that requires vigilance without rigidity, care without possession, and strength without domination."

Silence returned—not heavy, not hollow—but balanced.

Bhavya lowered her eyes, as if something within her had finally found the pressure it needed to rest.

In Buddha Hall, the gentle hand was no longer a concept.
It was a way of being— present, responsive, and willing to let life remain alive.

The light in **Buddha Hall** had begun to mellow, losing its sharpness as noon approached. Sunlight filtered through the high openings at a gentler angle now, warming the stone floor without urgency. Time itself seemed to loosen, aware that a pause was near—not an ending, but a breathing space.

The seekers remained seated, though bodies had begun to signal their humanity: a subtle shift of weight, a deeper inhale, the quiet recognition of hunger—not only for food, but for rest and assimilation. The questions of the morning had not burdened them; they had *worked* them, like soil turned patiently by hand.

Guruji sensed the rhythm changing.

He did not rush to conclude. He allowed the moment to ripen, just as he had allowed silence to ripen earlier. His eyes moved gently across the hall, resting on faces that no longer searched for answers but held them loosely, as one holds water in cupped palms.

Then he spoke—softly, deliberately.

From Judgment to Care

"Most ethical traditions," Guruji said, "begin with judgment."

The words landed calmly, without accusation.

"They ask who is right, who is wrong, who should be blamed, and who should be corrected."

He paused, letting the familiar framework reveal its limits.

"These questions belong to a world that imagines actions as separate and consequences as linear. But you have seen today—this is not how reality moves."

A quiet stillness settled, attentive but unstrained.

"When harm arises from systems," Guruji continued, "judgment becomes clumsy. It strikes individuals while leaving the deeper patterns untouched. It may satisfy our need for closure, but it rarely brings healing."

He opened his palm slightly, as if offering an alternative rather than insisting on one.

"Care asks different questions."

The hall seemed to lean in.

"Care asks: *What conditions allowed this to arise? What relationships failed to hold? What feedback was ignored?*"

He let the words breathe.

"To care is not to excuse harm," Guruji said gently. "It is to take responsibility for the whole terrain in which harm becomes possible."

A few heads bowed—not in agreement, but in recognition.

"Ethics in an emergent world," he continued, "is less like a courtroom and more like cultivation. You do not shout at a wilting plant. You study the soil, the water, the season, the invisible imbalances beneath the surface."

A faint softness moved through the room.

"This kind of ethics does not isolate blame—it distributes responsibility. It reminds us that none of us stands outside the system. We are participants, whether we choose to be conscious of it or not."

He paused again, sensing the natural closure forming—not an ending of thought, but a resting point.

"To move from judgment to care," Guruji said, "is to accept that our task is not to control outcomes, but to tend conditions. To protect the space in which healthier patterns can emerge."

Outside, the sound of distant movement—footsteps, utensils, the quiet life of the ashram preparing for the midday meal—drifted faintly into awareness, grounding the moment.

Guruji folded his palms softly.

"Let these reflections rest within you," he said. "Not as conclusions, but as nourishment. Understanding, like the body, needs time to digest."

He smiled—warm, human, unhurried.

"We will continue after the meal."

Silence followed—not heavy, not expectant—complete.

And in **Buddha Hall**, as the seekers slowly prepared to rise, it was clear: the teaching had not paused.

It had simply changed form—

from thought to breath,

from insight to digestion,

from wisdom to life.

CHAPTER V

Futures of Coherence

"The same road leads to harmony or collapse, depending on how it is walked."

– Shree Shambav.

Synopsis

As emergent systems scale, their consequences extend beyond local failures toward civilizational and planetary stakes. This chapter explores how coherence itself becomes a source of existential risk—when tightly coupled systems amplify errors faster than they can be corrected. Traditional risk models, built on isolated events, falter in the face of emergent uncertainty.

The chapter then confronts a deeper question: does the universe trend toward complexity and meaning, or is this narrative a projection of human cognition onto thermodynamic drift? By holding emergent optimism alongside entropy-driven pessimism, the chapter resists simplistic conclusions.

Spiritual experience is reframed as a subjective recognition of coherence—moments when the self perceives its embeddedness in larger patterns. Finally, the chapter examines utopian and dystopian trajectories shaped by emerging technologies, arguing that the future of coherence depends not on prediction, but on ethical leverage points that nurture adaptability, restraint, and shared meaning.

The **Buddha Hall** rested in a luminous hush. Afternoon light spilled through the tall windows and settled gently upon the cool stone floor, illuminating drifting dust motes that floated like unclaimed thoughts—present, unhurried, waiting for meaning. The air still carried the softness of rest, the faint trace of nourishment, the aftertaste of silence that follows when the body has been tended, and the mind allowed to loosen its grip.

After the midday meal and a brief, restorative pause, the devotees returned—not as they had arrived in the morning with questions sharpened by curiosity, but as one returns to a river after crossing a long stretch of land: slower, quieter, inwardly attuned. Their footsteps were fewer than sounds; their movements seemed guided by listening rather than intention. Cushions were adjusted without urgency. Spines found their own alignment. Breaths settled into a shared rhythm, like waves learning one another's timing.

The hall did not fill with motion or murmurs. It is filled with **readiness**.

Guruji entered without ceremony and took his asana. He did not acknowledge the gathering with words or gestures. He simply *arrived.* His presence moved through the hall the way shade moves across a field—cooling, clarifying, asking nothing. He sat, eyes resting gently, hands open upon his knees, as though receiving the moment rather than occupying it.

He did not speak at once.

His stillness itself seemed to listen—to the breath of the room, to the faint residue of morning discourse, to the unspoken questions that had not yet found language. Silence gathered naturally, not imposed, not instructed, but drawn together like birds settling at dusk, instinctively aware that something essential was about to unfold.

When Guruji finally spoke, his voice carried a gravity that did not press downward but drew the heart inward, like gravity drawing water back to its source.

"This," he said softly, "is the moment many traditions gesture toward—but few pause long enough to see."

The words entered the hall without disturbance. They did not ask for agreement. They asked for presence.

He allowed the silence to absorb them.

"So much of human thought," Guruji continued, "is occupied with origins—where things come from—or with endings—how they collapse, conclude, or are resolved. But the most consequential moment is often neither the beginning nor the end."

He lifted his gaze slowly, letting it move across the room.

"It is the *edge*."

A subtle stillness deepened.

"The edge where patterns are forming faster than wisdom can stabilise them. Where power outpaces discernment. Where coherence is possible—but not guaranteed."

He paused again, as though giving the idea time to take root.

Futures of Coherence

"Emergence," Guruji said, "is not inherently benevolent. Nor is it inherently destructive. It is *amplifying*."

His voice remained calm, but its clarity carried weight.

"What it amplifies depends on what feeds it—attention, incentives, fear, care, impatience, restraint."

He made a small circular gesture with his hand, as if tracing an invisible spiral.

"A fire can warm a village or consume a forest. The difference is not the flame—it is the conditions surrounding it."

The hall felt suddenly vast, as though the walls had receded.

"We now stand in a time," Guruji continued, "where emergent systems—technological, social, ecological—are no longer local. Their effects ripple across continents, generations, and inner lives. Small decisions now echo with disproportionate force."

He let the words settle as stones dropped into deep water.

"This is not a moment of simple progress," he said. "It is a moment of *becoming*."

Opening Reflection – Standing at the Edge of Becoming

Guruji leaned forward slightly—not in urgency, but in intimacy.

"To stand at the edge of becoming is to recognise that the future is not a destination waiting for us. It is a pattern we are already shaping—often without realising it."

Outside the hall, a breeze moved through the trees, rustling leaves like distant applause or warning—it was impossible to tell which.

"Emergent power," Guruji said, "does not ask permission. It grows wherever conditions allow it. The question before us is not whether coherence will emerge—but *what kind*."

He held the silence again.

"Will coherence amplify wisdom—or volatility? Will it deepen care—or accelerate fragmentation? Will it bind us into larger harmonies—or lock us into self-reinforcing loops of fear and control?"

No one shifted. No one reached for an answer.

"This is why the future of coherence is not a technical problem alone," Guruji said softly. "It is an ethical, relational, and attentional one."

His eyes rested gently on the group.

"The systems you inherit will shape you. The systems you participate in will shape others. And the systems you ignore will shape you anyway."

A few breaths passed.

"To stand at this edge," he said, "is to accept responsibility without pretending to mastery. To act without certainty. To cultivate conditions rather than dictate outcomes."

He fell silent.

The afternoon light continued its slow migration across the floor. Dust motes drifted, unclaimed, luminous. Somewhere beyond the hall, life went on—unaware, emergent, unfinished.

And within **Buddha Hall**, the seekers sat at the threshold—not of answers, but of awareness—feeling, perhaps for the first time, the quiet weight of standing not *after* history, but *inside* its becoming.

The afternoon in **Buddha Hall** had ripened into a deeper stillness. The sun, now higher, no longer poured itself in with generosity but filtered through the windows in narrow, deliberate shafts—as though even light had learned restraint. Outside, the world carried on with its quiet rhythms, yet inside the hall, something weightier had gathered. The earlier reflections on coherence and becoming had unsettled familiar ground. The questions were no longer academic. They touched the future. They touched survival.

Guruji sat unmoving, his presence steady, neither urgent nor detached. When he lifted his gaze, it was not toward any one devotee, but toward the shared horizon of concern that now filled the room.

Sofia spoke, her voice careful, carrying both curiosity and unease.

"Guruji," she asked, "do coherent emergent properties—like artificial general intelligence, climate engineering, or global techno-social networks—create *unique* catastrophic risks? How do we weigh these emergent uncertainties when traditional risk models depend on linear prediction and known variables?"

The question did not seek reassurance. It sought orientation.

Guruji did not answer immediately. He allowed the silence to expand, as if making space for the magnitude of what had been named. Then he spoke, slowly.

Emergent Existential Risks

"Most dangers humanity has faced," Guruji began, "arrived like storms—visible on the horizon, measurable in force, local in consequence. You could see them coming. You could build walls. You could flee."

He paused, his fingers lightly touching the floor beside his asana.

"Emergent risks," he continued, "arrive differently. They do not roar. They *converge.*"

The word settled heavily.

"AGI, climate engineering, planetary-scale networks—these are not single tools or isolated inventions. They are *coherent systems* that learn, adapt, and amplify their own patterns. Their danger lies not in what they do intentionally, but in what they make possible unintentionally."

He looked toward the far wall, where sunlight traced a thin line across the stone.

"Traditional risk models assume independence—one cause, one effect, one probability curve. Emergent systems violate this assumption. Causes loop back on themselves. Effects reshape the system that produced them. Prediction collapses not because we lack data, but because the system is changing *while* we observe it."

The Storm Without a Sky

Guruji offered an analogy.

"Imagine," he said, "a river that suddenly learns how to redirect its own flow. Not consciously—but structurally. Each bend reshapes the next current.

Now ask yourself: where would you place a dam? What measurement would tell you when the flood begins?"

A few devotees shifted—not in discomfort, but in recognition.

"Existential risk," Guruji said, "emerges when coherence reaches a scale where small misalignments propagate faster than correction can occur."

He turned gently toward Sofia.

"Climate engineering is not dangerous because it is powerful. It is dangerous because it couples planetary systems that evolved independently. AGI is not risky because it thinks. It is risky because it may optimise coherence in directions orthogonal to human values—without malice, without rebellion, without pause."

Beyond the Calculus of Control

Guruji's voice softened, but its clarity sharpened.

"You ask how to *weigh* emergent uncertainties. The truth is—some risks cannot be weighed. They must be *held*."

He lifted one hand, palm upward, as if cradling something fragile.

"Linear models ask, 'What is the probability of failure?' Emergent ethics must ask, 'What is the *irreversibility* of error?'"

The hall felt suddenly very quiet.

"When a bridge collapses, it can be rebuilt. When a self-modifying global system crosses a threshold, there may be no outside left to intervene."

He allowed that to rest.

"This is why emergent existential risk is not merely a statistical problem—it is a moral one. It forces humility. It demands precaution not as fear, but as wisdom."

The Edge That Cannot Be Uncrossed

Guruji leaned slightly forward.

"Emergent systems often fail *gracefully*—until they do not. For a long time, feedback appears manageable. Adjustments seem sufficient. And then, quietly, a boundary is crossed."

He drew an invisible line in the air.

"Beyond that line, the system's own coherence resists correction. It protects its pattern."

He looked at the group.

"The danger is not a catastrophe by explosion. It is a catastrophe by *lock-in*."

A New Kind of Responsibility

"Therefore," Guruji said, "the question is not how much risk we can tolerate—but what kinds of futures we are willing to make *unrecoverable*."

Silence held the hall.

"To live wisely in an age of emergent power," he said, "is to design slowly, to monitor deeply, and to preserve the option to stop. Not everything that can be stabilised should be. Not every coherence should be scaled."

His gaze softened.

"The highest responsibility is not prediction. It is restraint."

Sofia lowered her eyes, not in resignation, but in understanding.

The light outside shifted again. Somewhere, a bell rang faintly in the distance. Inside **Buddha Hall**, the devotees remained still—aware now that the future was not a distant abstraction, but a fragile coherence already taking shape around them, asking not for certainty, but for care.

The afternoon had begun to lean toward evening, though the sun still lingered, reluctant to leave. In **Buddha Hall**, the air carried a subtle heaviness—not of fatigue, but of gravity. The earlier reflections on emergent risks had loosened something inside the listeners, as snow disturbed high on a silent mountain. No sound yet. No collapse yet. Only awareness that the slope was steeper than it appeared.

Guruji remained seated, his presence unbroken. Outside, somewhere beyond the hall, the world continued to hum—networks pulsing, markets breathing, machines conversing with machines. Inside, the devotees sat as if listening not only to him, but to the future pressing gently against the present.

Bhavya spoke, his voice steady but edged with concern.

"Guruji," he asked, "how do emergent risks differ from traditional hazards? And why do they demand new forms of foresight—and humility?"

Guruji's eyes rested on Bhavya for a moment, not to answer him, but to include him fully in the question. Then he began.

The Invisible Avalanche

"Traditional hazards," Guruji said, "announce themselves."

He paused, letting the words find their shape.

"A storm darkens the sky. An earthquake shakes the ground. A fire reveals itself through heat and smoke. These dangers are immediate, sensory, and local. They frighten us—but they also warn us."

He lifted his gaze toward the high ceiling of the hall.

"Emergent risks do not warn. They *accumulate*."

The devotees leaned in, almost imperceptibly.

"They arise not from force, but from *coupling*. From systems bound so tightly together that a minor disturbance cannot dissipate—it must travel."

Snow That Moves in Silence

Guruji offered an image.

"High in the mountains," he said, "snow settles one flake at a time. Each flake is harmless. Each one believes it rests alone. But together, under the right conditions, they form a mass that remembers every slope, every tension, every imbalance."

He drew a slow breath.

"An avalanche does not begin when the mountain breaks. It begins when the *relationships* between flakes become unstable."

A quiet understanding passed through the hall.

"So it is with global systems today. A small feedback error—an algorithmic misalignment, a delayed signal, a localised optimisation—can cascade through financial networks, climate systems, information flows, and automated decision structures."

He looked at Bhavya.

"No single component fails. The system fails *coherently.*"

Why We Do Not See It Coming

"Traditional hazards," Guruji continued, "operate in straight lines. Cause leads to effect. Damage remains proportional. Recovery, though painful, is imaginable."

His voice lowered.

"Emergent hazards bend time and scale. They turn delays into accelerants. They transform correction into amplification."

He raised his hand slightly, tracing a loop in the air.

"Feedback, when misunderstood, becomes fate."

The room felt still, but not empty.

"These risks escape our notice because each local decision appears rational. Each optimisation works—until they synchronise."

The Illusion of Control

Bhavya listened intently as Guruji spoke again.

"We were trained to believe that mastery comes from precision," Guruji said. "That if we measure finely enough, regulate tightly enough, predict deeply enough, we can command outcomes."

A faint sadness touched his voice.

"Emergent systems humble this belief. They reveal that control, when applied without reverence, becomes the very trigger of collapse."

He leaned forward slightly.

"When systems are tightly coupled, there is no room for error—and therefore no room for learning. Failure becomes instantaneous."

A New Kind of Foresight

"So what kind of foresight is required?" Guruji asked, answering Bhavya's question by turning it inward.

"Not professional foresight alone. Not better dashboards or faster simulations."

He paused.

"We need *ethical foresight*—the ability to sense when coherence is outpacing wisdom."

His gaze moved slowly across the hall.

"This means designing systems that can fail gently. That can pause. That can be questioned. That leaves space for human judgment, slowness, and doubt."

Why Humility Is No Longer Optional

Guruji's voice softened, but its weight deepened.

"Humility," he said, "is not weakness in an emergent world. It is structural safety."

He gestured lightly, as if holding something delicate.

"To admit that we do not fully understand a system is to resist sealing it too tightly. To accept uncertainty is to preserve the option of retreat."

He looked again at Bhavya.

“Emergent risks demand humility because they punish arrogance silently—and all at once.”

The Avalanche Has No Villain

Guruji said quietly.

“When an avalanche descends, no snowflake is guilty. No single choice is immoral. Yet destruction follows.”

He let the silence speak.

“In the age we are entering, wisdom lies not in asking who is to blame—but in learning how to walk lightly on slopes we do not fully understand.”

The light outside had begun to fade. Shadows lengthened across the stone floor of **Buddha Hall**. The devotees remained still, aware now that the greatest dangers of their time might not arrive with noise or fire—but with quiet, invisible coherence, already in motion beneath their feet.

Outside, a breeze moved through the trees, carrying with it the faint rustle of impermanence. Inside, the hall breathed slowly, holding the weight of questions that did not seek quick answers.

Divyani spoke from a place of quiet wonder rather than doubt.

"Guruji," she asked, "is emergence evidence of a cosmic direction—or is it a narrative scaffold we humans build to make sense of impermanence?"

The question did not ripple through the hall. It settled—like an arrow laid gently on the ground, waiting to be examined rather than fired.

Guruji closed his eyes for a moment, as though listening not only to Divyani, but to time itself. When he opened them, there was neither certainty nor dismissal in his gaze—only spaciousness.

The Arrow We Draw

"Watch the smoke from an oil lamp," Guruji began.

Several lamps still flickered along the walls, their flames steady, their smoke barely visible.

"It rises," he said, "twisting upward, forming delicate patterns—brief, beautiful, unmistakably ordered. And yet, no matter how graceful its ascent, it eventually disperses into the vastness of the air."

He let the image linger.

"This," he said, "is the paradox you are pointing toward."

Local Order, Global Dissolution

Guruji's voice carried a calm clarity.

"Emergence is real," he said. "Complexity does arise. Atoms become molecules. Molecules learn to sing as cells. Cells remember how to become forests, minds, civilisations."

A faint smile crossed his face.

"Within small pockets of the universe, coherence blooms—like islands of meaning in an ocean of entropy."

He lifted a finger slightly, not to argue, but to balance.

"But entropy does not retreat. It does not negotiate. While complexity increases locally, disorder continues its quiet expansion globally."

The devotees felt it—not as despair, but as truth.

"The universe," Guruji said, "does not promise permanence. It allows *patterns*."

The Human Need for Direction

Divyani listened intently as Guruji continued.

“Humans,” he said gently, “are meaning-making beings. We cannot bear chaos without a story. So when we observe emergence, we draw an arrow through it.”

He traced an invisible line in the air.

“We call it progress. Evolution. Destiny. Awakening.”

His voice softened.

“These stories are not lies—but they are *frames*. They help us stand upright in a world that constantly dissolves beneath our feet.”

Is the Arrow in the Cosmos—or in Us?

Guruji paused, allowing the question to turn inward.

“Does the universe intend complexity?” he asked quietly. “Or does complexity simply arise wherever conditions briefly allow it—like frost forming on a window at dawn?”

He looked toward the fading light.

“The cosmos does not declare its purpose. It does not announce a direction. It unfolds.”

He turned back to Divyani.

"The arrow you see may not belong to the universe—it may belong to the *witness*."

Emergence as a Temporary Mercy

Guruji's voice grew tender.

"Emergence may not be a promise of permanence," he said. "It may be a mercy—a temporary stay against dissolution."

He gestured toward the hall itself.

"This hall, these bodies, these thoughts—each is a momentary coherence borrowed from chaos."

The devotees felt the weight and the gift of it.

"To see emergence as cosmic destiny can inflate us. To see it as an illusion can hollow us. Wisdom lies between."

Living Without Certainty, But With Care

"So how should we live?" Guruji asked softly.

"Not as if the universe guarantees meaning. And not as if meaning is pointless."

He met Divyani's eyes.

"We live as gardeners in borrowed soil—knowing the garden will not last forever, yet tending it with devotion."

The Arrow as Responsibility, Not Proof

Guruji said:

"Whether emergence points toward a cosmic direction or reflects our longing to survive impermanence is finally undecidable."

He let silence complete the thought.

"But the arrow we draw need not prove destiny. It needs only guide *care*."

Outside, the sun slipped lower, surrendering the sky to evening. Inside **Buddha Hall**, the devotees sat quietly, understanding that meaning might not be written into the universe—but entrusted to those who momentarily awaken within it.

The hall felt less like a place and more like a field—subtle, attentive, alive with quiet expectancy.

The devotees sat unmoving, but inwardly stirred. The earlier discourses on emergence, risk, and coherence had unsettled old certainties—not violently, but like a river loosening stones that had long believed themselves to be ground. In that openness, Kieron spoke.

His voice carried reverence, not scepticism.

"Guruji," he asked, "can spiritual experiences—like awe, unity, or a sense of interconnectedness—be understood as subjective recognition of cosmic coherence? And if so, does that make them merely natural… or does it deepen their significance?"

The question seemed to expand the room rather than occupy it.

Guruji did not answer immediately. He looked toward the far wall, where light and shadow touched without conflict. Then he turned back, his eyes reflecting something both ancient and immediate.

Spirituality as Coherence Recognition

"Have you ever watched a flock of birds turn in the sky?" Guruji asked softly.

Several devotees nodded. Some smiled.

"They move," he continued, "as though guided by a single intelligence—yet there is no commander, no signal, no central will. Each bird follows simple rules, responding only to its nearest neighbours. And yet… what emerges is breathtaking."

He paused.

"When you witness that," he asked, "do you feel awe?"

Kieron nodded slowly.

"That awe," Guruji said, "is not superstition. It is *recognition*."

Not Intervention, but Alignment

"Spiritual experience," Guruji continued, "is often misunderstood as something added to reality—as if the universe briefly breaks its own laws to whisper secrets into our ears."

A faint smile crossed his face.

"But what if spirituality is not interruption, but *alignment*?"

The hall grew still.

"What if," he said, "a spiritual moment is simply consciousness becoming sensitive enough to perceive coherence that was always there?"

The Veil Thinning

Guruji leaned forward slightly.

"Most of the time," he said, "we live inside fragments. We see ourselves as separate—mind against body, self against world, now against future."

He held his hands apart, then slowly brought them closer.

"But sometimes—through silence, suffering, love, beauty, or exhaustion—the boundaries thin."

His voice softened.

"And suddenly, the fragments remember they belong to a whole."

A Story from the Riverbank

Guruji's gaze drifted inward, as though recalling something lived rather than imagined.

"There was once a man," he said, "who stood every morning beside a river. He bathed in it, drank from it, crossed it, cursed it when it flooded, thanked it when it sustained his crops."

The devotees listened.

"One day," Guruji continued, "he stood still for a long time, watching the water move. Not using it. Not naming it. Just watching."

He paused.

"And in that moment, he felt something he had never felt before—not that the river was divine, but that *he had never been separate from its movement.*"

The hall breathed.

"Nothing supernatural happened," Guruji said. "The river did not speak. The sky did not open."

He smiled gently.

"But the man was changed forever."

Natural Does Not Mean Shallow

Guruji turned back to Kieron.

"So you ask—does framing spirituality as emergent phenomenology make it less sacred?"

He shook his head slowly.

"To say that love arises from neurochemistry does not make love small. To say music arises from vibrations does not make music hollow."

His voice deepened.

"To understand *how* something arises does not exhaust *what it means.*"

The Depth of Recognition

"When consciousness recognises coherence," Guruji said, "it is not inventing meaning. It is *remembering participation*."

He placed his hand lightly on his chest.

"That recognition carries ethical weight. Humility. Care. Responsibility."

The devotees felt it—this was not abstraction.

"Awe is not an emotion," Guruji continued. "It is a posture of the self when it realises it is not the centre."

Spirituality Reclaimed

"So yes," Guruji said softly, "spiritual experience can be understood as subjective recognition of cosmic coherence."

He let the words settle.

"And no," he added, "this does not diminish it."

His eyes moved slowly across the hall.

"It deepens it—because it asks more of us."

Outside, the evening wind stirred the trees. Inside **Buddha Hall**, something subtle had aligned—not a belief, not a doctrine, but a recognition. That spirituality was not an escape from the world… but a moment of seeing how intimately one belonged to it.

The question arose not abruptly, but the way dew forms—quietly, inevitably—on a morning that has already softened the world.

Astyn spoke from that listening.

"Guruji," he asked, his voice steady yet tender, "are spiritual experiences merely neural events—patterns of firing neurons and chemistry? Or do they represent a lived recognition of emergent coherence across scales?"

The words lingered like incense, dissolving slowly.

Guruji did not respond at once. His eyes closed briefly—not in withdrawal, but in attunement. When he opened them, there was no urgency in his gaze, only a quiet precision.

The Moment of Awe

"In rare moments," Guruji said, "the mind loosens its grip on separation."

He paused.

"And in that loosening, something vast is allowed to be felt."

The Instrument and the Music

"Tell me," he continued gently, "when a veena vibrates, where does the music live?"

A few devotees exchanged glances.

"In the strings?" Guruji asked.

"In the wood?"

"In the air that carries the sound?"

He smiled softly.

"The nervous system," he said, "is the *instrument* of experience. But no one mistakes the instrument for the music."

Neural Fire, Cosmic Pattern

"Yes," Guruji said plainly, "every spiritual experience has a neural signature. Just as every sunrise has a spectrum, and every ocean wave has a frequency."

He lifted his hand slightly, as though tracing an unseen arc.

"But the presence of a mechanism does not exhaust the meaning of the pattern it enables."

The hall seemed to lean forward.

"When the brain quiets habitual prediction," Guruji continued, "when the self-model softens, when boundaries dissolve—what emerges is not hallucination."

His voice deepened.

"It is *coherence becoming perceptible.*"

A Story of the Bell

"There was once a monastery," Guruji said, "where a bell was rung at dawn."

The devotees settled into the story.

"One morning, a young monk asked the elder, 'Is the bell calling us to prayer, or are we calling meaning into the sound?'"

Guruji smiled.

"The elder struck the bell again and said, 'The bell does not summon silence. Silence reveals the bell.'"

He let that settle.

"So it is with awe," Guruji said. "The experience does not create coherence. It reveals it."

Across Scales, Not Outside Nature

"During moments of awe," Guruji continued, "the mind stops insisting that meaning must be *local*—confined to the self, the body, the story we tell about 'me.'"

He gestured outward, then inward.

"One feels continuity across scales—cell to body, body to breath, breath to world, world to cosmos."

His voice softened.

"Not because one has travelled anywhere—but because the illusion of isolation has momentarily relaxed."

Not Reduction, but Completion

Astyn listened intently.

"So are these moments merely neural events?" Guruji asked, echoing the question.

He shook his head.

"They are *neural events precisely because recognition must occur somewhere*. But they are not *merely* neural, just as a map is not merely ink."

The hall felt warmer, though no lamps had changed.

"To reduce awe to chemistry," Guruji said, "is like reducing love to hormones—accurate in description, false in conclusion."

The Ethics of Awe

"When separation dissolves," Guruji said, "responsibility expands."

His tone grew serious, but gentle.

"One who has tasted coherence finds it difficult to exploit without consequence. One who has felt belonging cannot easily justify domination."

A quiet understanding moved through the hall.

"That," Guruji said, "is why spiritual experience matters—not as belief, but as *reorientation*."

The Quiet After Recognition

Guruji fell silent.

No one rushed to fill the space.

Astyn felt something subtle settle—not an answer to be stored, but a perspective to be lived.

The question arrived like a crossroads revealed at twilight.

Buddha Hall was no longer flooded with light, nor surrendered to darkness. Evening had braided the two together. Lamps had been lit along the pillars, their flames steady yet alive, casting halos rather than shadows. The air carried a faint coolness now, as if the day itself had exhaled. Outside, distant bells from the temple town echoed softly, reminders that the world beyond the hall was still turning, choosing, becoming.

Espen spoke from the middle of the circle, his voice thoughtful, unhurried.

"Guruji," he asked, "will emerging technologies amplify coherence—creating global symbiosis—or will they fracture it, deepening polarisation and control? What leverage points might tip the balance?"

The words settled heavily, not because they were dramatic, but because they were already unfolding in the world beyond these walls.

Guruji remained still for a long moment. His gaze moved slowly across the hall—not to meet eyes, but to sense the field of attention itself. When he spoke, his voice was low, steady, neither hopeful nor grim.

Utopian and Dystopian Pathways

"The future," Guruji said, "is not a destination waiting for us."

He paused.

"It is a *direction we keep reinforcing.*"

The Same River, Two Shores

"Consider a river," Guruji continued. "Its water is neither benevolent nor cruel. It carries nutrients—and it can drown. It irrigates fields—and it can erode villages."

He lifted his hand slightly, as if tracing a flowing line.

"The difference is not the river. It is the *relationship* between the river and the land."

The devotees listened intently.

"Emergent technologies," Guruji said, "are rivers of unprecedented speed and volume. Data, intelligence, automation—these are currents, not intentions."

He looked toward Espen.

"Utopia and dystopia are not opposite technologies. They are opposite *alignments*."

The Dialectic of Amplification

"Emergence amplifies what already exists," Guruji said. "It does not create values—it magnifies them."

His voice deepened.

"A system trained on fear scales fear. A system optimised for profit scales extraction. A system embedded in trust scales cooperation."

The hall felt very still.

"This is why the same algorithm can connect distant cultures—or lock them into mutually hostile echo chambers."

A Story of the Mirror City

"There is an old story," Guruji said, "of a city built entirely of mirrors."

The devotees leaned in.

"Every street reflected every face. Every house multiplied every gesture. A smile became a thousand smiles. A frown became a crowd of shadows."

He paused.

"At first, the people celebrated. 'Look,' they said, 'how visible we are.'"

"But soon," Guruji continued, "they realised something terrifying: the city did not *change* them. It revealed them—at scale."

Some shifted uneasily.

"The city was neither utopia nor dystopia," Guruji said softly. "It was an amplifier."

Leverage Points: Where the Dial Turns

Espen listened closely as Guruji's tone sharpened—not with force, but with clarity.

"The balance tips," Guruji said, "not at the level of tools—but at three quieter thresholds."

He raised one finger.

"First: **incentives**.

Systems follow rewards, not intentions. If outrage is rewarded, outrage becomes efficient. If care is rewarded, care becomes scalable."

A second finger.

"Second: **feedback speed**.

When harm travels faster than accountability, systems destabilise. When feedback is immediate and humane, coherence has a chance to self-correct."

A third finger.

"And third: **who is allowed to adapt**.

Rigid systems fracture. Systems that distribute agency—allowing local wisdom to adjust global patterns—tend toward resilience."

Neither Salvation nor Doom

"Do not ask," Guruji said gently, "whether technology will save us or destroy us."

His gaze softened.

"Ask instead: *what kind of coherence are we feeding?*"

He leaned slightly forward.

"Because emergence does not choose sides. It chooses *consistency*."

The Inner Technology

After a pause, Guruji added quietly,

"There is one technology older than all others."

The devotees waited.

"Attention."

He smiled faintly.

"Where we place it determines what grows. At planetary scale, this truth does not disappear—it becomes dangerous to ignore."

Silence returned—not empty, but charged.

Espen did not feel answered in the way the mind prefers. Instead, he felt entrusted—with responsibility rather than prediction.

Outside, the lamps flickered in the evening breeze. Somewhere beyond Buddha Hall, servers hummed, markets shifted, and algorithms learned. And within the stillness of the hall, the devotees sensed the unsettling truth:

The future was not approaching them.

They were already participating in it—breath by breath, choice by choice—turning the dial, often without knowing their hand was on it.

Greta's question rose gently from the stillness, but it carried the weight of a knife's edge.

"Guruji," she asked, "what leverage points—ethical, institutional, or cultural—might tip emergent futures toward coherence rather than fracture?"

Guruji did not answer immediately. He looked at the central lamp, its flame dancing yet unbroken. Then he spoke, his voice soft but exact, like a hand finding a pulse.

The Tipping Thread

The same technology unites—or divides.

"Every complex system," Guruji began, "rests on threads thinner than we imagine."

He gestured toward the flame.

"A flame stands not because of strength, but because balance is continuously renewed. Too much fuel, and it chokes. Too little, and it dies."

He looked back at the circle.

"Emergent futures are the same. They do not collapse from catastrophe alone. They tip when a subtle balance is ignored for too long."

A Weaver's Story

"In a village long ago," Guruji said, "there lived a master weaver. He taught his students that the cloth does not fail when a rope snaps—but when a single thread is neglected."

The devotees listened, breath slow.

"One day, a student asked, 'Which thread is most important?'"

Guruji smiled faintly.

"The weaver replied, 'The one you think is too small to matter.'"

Ethical Leverage: What We Normalise

"Ethics," Guruji said, "is not primarily about rules. It is about what becomes normal."

His voice deepened.

"When surveillance becomes ordinary, trust thins.

When speed outruns reflection, wisdom lags behind.

When efficiency replaces care, people become variables."

He paused.

"Emergent systems magnify norms. What is tolerated today becomes infrastructure tomorrow."

The hall felt very still.

"Ethical leverage," Guruji continued, "lies in refusing to normalise what corrodes dignity—even when it is convenient."

Institutional Leverage: Who Holds the Feedback

"Institutions," Guruji said, "are memory made durable."

He turned slightly, as if addressing an invisible architecture.

"They decide whose suffering is visible, whose voice loops back into correction, and whose pain is absorbed as 'externality.'"

He spoke more slowly now.

"Systems fracture when feedback is delayed, deflected, or denied. They heal when correction is not punished—but welcomed."

Greta felt something tighten in her chest.

"An institution that cannot admit error," Guruji said softly, "will force reality to do it for them—violently."

Cultural Leverage: What We Teach Children Without Words

Culture, Guruji explained, was the deepest thread of all.

"Culture is not what we declare," he said. "It is what children learn without being told."

He glanced around the hall.

"Do they learn competition or cooperation?

Do they learn to listen—or to perform?

Do they learn that worth is intrinsic—or conditional?"

He paused, letting the questions breathe.

"Technologies follow culture the way water follows terrain."

The Narrow Bridge

Guruji leaned slightly forward.

"The future does not need perfect people," he said. "It needs sensitive systems."

He raised his hand, thumb and forefinger close.

"There is a narrow bridge between coherence and fracture. On one side is rigidity—control, certainty, domination. On the other is chaos—neglect, fragmentation, indifference."

He lowered his hand.

"The bridge is walked by humility."

The Final Thread

Greta watched the flame as Guruji said.

"The greatest leverage point," he said quietly, "is whether we treat emergence as something to command—or something to care for."

He smiled gently.

"Care is not weakness. It is skilled attention sustained over time."

Silence returned, deep and warm.

The devotees did not feel instructed—they felt entrusted. Somewhere beyond Buddha Hall, the same technologies Greta had spoken of were linking strangers, polarising nations, and accelerating choices. But here, in this stillness, a quieter truth settled:

The future would not be tipped by grand declarations.

It would turn—slowly, decisively—on the threads people chose to notice, protect, and weave with care.

Guruji remained seated for a long moment after the last question had dissolved into stillness. His eyes were half-closed, not withdrawn from the room, but resting within it.

Choosing Conditions, Not Outcomes

Guruji said softly, "Humanity has always tried to command the future by naming its destination. We draw maps of what *must* happen, then suffer when life refuses to follow our lines."

He paused, letting the weight of recognition move through the hall.

"Outcomes," he continued, "are seductive. They promise certainty. But in complex worlds, certainty is an illusion borrowed from simpler times."

He gestured gently, as if tracing the air.

"Consider the farmer. He does not order the seed to become a tree. He prepares the soil, protects it from erosion, ensures water and sunlight, and then—he waits. Growth happens not because he commands it, but because he *respects the conditions that allow it.*"

A few devotees nodded slowly, as if remembering something they had always known.

The Error of Force

"When we obsess over endpoints," Guruji said, "we tighten our grip. And tightened systems lose sensitivity."

His voice was calm, but there was gravity in it.

"Control narrows feedback. It silences weak signals. It mistakes compliance for coherence."

He let the words breathe.

"Many failures—technological, social, even spiritual—do not occur because intentions were evil. They occur because systems were forced toward outcomes faster than they could adapt."

Conditions as Silent Architects

Guruji looked around the hall, meeting faces without fixing on any one.

"Conditions," he said, "are invisible architects. They shape behaviour long before choice becomes conscious."

He spoke gently now.

"Change the incentives, and values follow.

Change the rhythms, and attention reshapes itself.

Change what is rewarded, and identity reorganises."

He smiled faintly.

"People believe they are choosing freely, not realising the ground beneath them has already been tilted."

The Humility of Not Knowing

"To choose conditions," Guruji continued, "requires humility—the courage to admit we do not fully know what the future *should* look like."

A quiet settled in the hall, deeper than before.

"This humility is not weakness," he said. "It is alignment with reality."

He closed his eyes briefly.

"When we stop insisting on outcomes, we regain the capacity to listen. And listening is how coherence reveals its next step."

The Ethical Shift

"Ethics, then," Guruji said, opening his eyes, "is no longer about prescribing final states. It becomes an ongoing act of cultivation."

His voice softened.

"Protect diversity so adaptation remains possible.

Preserve feedback so correction remains gentle.

Nurture trust so coordination does not require force."

He looked toward the central lamp again.

"This is how futures are chosen—not through domination, but through care sustained across time."

The Seed Left Unnamed

Guruji fell silent.

No ritual followed. No closing gesture was made.

The devotees sat with the feeling that something had been placed quietly within them—not an answer, but a responsibility. The future, they sensed, was not a distant horizon waiting to be reached. It was already forming, moment by moment, in the conditions they allowed, ignored, or protected.

The lamps continued to burn.

And in their steady light, the truth settled without demand:

The most powerful choice humanity holds

is not *where* it is going—

but *how* it prepares the ground for what wishes to emerge.

CHAPTER VI

Coherent Emergentism

"A philosophy is tested not by its elegance, but by the kind of lives it makes possible."

– Shree Shambav.

Synopsis

This final chapter synthesises the book's central argument: emergence is not merely a scientific concept but a way of orienting thought, ethics, and action. Coherent emergentism is presented as a unifying framework capable of integrating physics, biology, mind, society, and value without reducing higher-level phenomena to their parts or invoking metaphysical dualism.

Rather than "solving" the explanatory gaps surrounding consciousness and meaning, the framework reframes them as natural consequences of layered organisation—features to be understood relationally rather than eliminated. By emphasising coherence across domains, emergentism offers an antidote to modern epistemic fragmentation, where knowledge advances in isolated silos divorced from ethical consequence.

The chapter concludes with a practical challenge: if coherent emergentism is true, truth itself demands behavioural expression. How we live, design systems, and relate to non-human entities becomes the ultimate test of whether coherence is merely discussed—or embodied.

After the evening break, the devotees returned to the Buddha Hall as though guided by a tide that required no moon. No one called them back. No bell summoned them. Yet one by one, and then in small constellations, they found themselves walking the familiar paths again—drawn not by habit, but by an unspoken pull that rose from within.

Outside, the world was quietly changing its attire.

The sky had deepened into a vast indigo, the kind that feels less like colour and more like depth. Stars appeared shyly at first—single points of light testing their courage—then multiplied, settling into patterns older than memory.

Night found its voice in layers.

Frogs called from the edges of water, steady and rhythmic, as if keeping time for the dark. Insects hummed like taut strings on an unseen instrument, vibrating with life. A solitary bird called once, then again, passing sound from shadow to shadow. A cool breeze threaded its way through the corridors, carrying the scent of damp earth and leaves, brushing against skin like a gentle reminder: the world, too, was awake—learning in its own language.

Inside the Buddha Hall, oil lamps glowed with quiet devotion. Their flames did not flicker wildly; they stood attentive, as though listening. Shadows settled along the walls, not restless but composed. The stone floor held the day's warmth, releasing it slowly, generously.

The devotees took their seats.

They did not arrive with eagerness alone, but with a certain inward ripeness. The questions of the day had not been answered so much as absorbed. Something had softened. Something had loosened its grip. Minds that once reached outward now rested more easily within. The hall did not feel full of people; it felt full of *readiness.*

After a few unmeasured minutes, Guruji entered.

There was no announcement. There never was.

Yet the room recognised him before thought could name the recognition. Conversations dissolved mid-breath. Spines aligned as if remembering an older posture. Breaths slowed—not by instruction, but by contagion. Presence adjusted itself around his presence, the way water reshapes without resistance when a stone is placed within it.

He walked to his asana with the unhurried ease of one who had never been in conflict with time. When he sat, silence spread outward—not as absence, not as command, but as life. It was the silence of a lake at dusk, holding the sky's reflection without effort, without commentary.

Guruji closed his eyes for a moment.

Even the night outside seemed to lean closer.

When he opened them and finally spoke, his voice did not assert—it *aligned.* It carried neither the sharpness of argument nor the weight of authority. It carried orientation, the way a compass carries north without insisting anyone follow.

"Emergence," Guruji said softly, "is often treated as an idea to be proven or debated. But it is neither hypothesis nor ornament."

He let the words settle.

"It is an *orientation.*"

The lamps seemed to glow a little steadier.

"We live in an age of fragments," he continued. "Science speaks one language, ethics in another.

Spirituality is placed on one side, daily life on the other. Knowledge is divided into disciplines that no longer recognise their shared roots. Each fragment is brilliant in isolation—and yet together, they fail to cohere."

His gaze moved slowly across the hall, not fixing on faces, but on the space between them.

"Coherent emergentism is not an attempt to force unity where none exists," he said. "It is an invitation to *notice* the unity that is already functioning beneath our divisions."

He paused, as though listening for something older than speech.

"A cell does not know it serves the body. A neuron does not know it participates in thought. A single ant does not comprehend the colony. And yet—from these unknowing parts—life, mind, and intelligence arise."

A soft stillness deepened.

"In the same way," Guruji continued, "your disciplines, your roles, your identities—scientist, seeker, parent, citizen—are not meant to agree at the level of control. They are meant to cohere at the level of *relation*."

He lifted his hand slightly, palm open.

"Emergentism, when understood coherently, is not a theory explaining how complexity appears. It is a lens through which fragmentation begins to heal. It reminds us that meaning is not imposed from above, nor manufactured from below—but *revealed* through relationship."

The night outside seemed to breathe with him.

"When we adopt this lens," he said, "science regains humility. Ethics regains depth. Spirituality regains grounding. And lived experience regains dignity—not as something separate from knowledge, but as its most intimate expression."

Silence followed—not the silence of confusion, but the silence that arrives when something aligns too deeply for immediate response.

In that stillness, the devotees felt it—not as agreement, not as conclusion—but as a quiet reorientation. Like realising the stars had never moved; only the gaze had.

And as the moon climbed higher outside the hall, casting silver patterns through the windows, the Buddha Hall held them all—parts and wholes, questions and quiet—resting together within a single, listening coherence.

The hall remained wrapped in the afterglow of Guruji's previous words. Lamps burned steadily now, as though they, too, had settled into understanding. Outside, night had fully claimed the sky, yet inside the Buddha Hall there was no sense of darkness—only depth. The kind of depth one feels when looking into a still well and realising the water is not empty, but reflective.

Akanksh shifted slightly, then folded his palms—not as formality, but as readiness. His voice, when it came, carried both curiosity and restraint, like someone stepping carefully onto sacred ground.

"Guruji," he asked, "can coherent emergentism truly unify science, philosophy, and ethics into a non-reductive cosmology? Or does it simply add another layer of complexity—another story competing with all the others?"

The question did not disturb the silence. It seemed to be complete it.

Guruji did not answer immediately. He looked toward the lamps, then beyond them, as though gazing through centuries rather than walls. When he finally spoke, his voice was soft, but it carried the weight of careful seeing.

"You are asking about the hunger beneath all thinking," he said. "The hunger for a story large enough to hold everything—without flattening anything."

He paused.

"Humanity has always lived by grand narratives. Some were spoken by myth. Some by religion. Some by science. When a narrative is alive, it does not dominate—it *orients*. When it decays, it becomes dogma."

A faint wind brushed through the hall, stirring the lamp flames.

"Reductionism gave us power," Guruji continued. "It taught us how to take the world apart with exquisite precision. But it forgot to ask a quieter question: once taken apart, *how does the whole return?*"

He turned his gaze back to the circle.

"Holism tried to answer this by declaring everything connected—but without structure, connection becomes fog. When everything means everything, nothing guides action."

A gentle murmur of recognition passed through the listeners.

"Coherent emergentism is not a new grand story competing with old ones," Guruji said. "It is an attempt to understand *how stories themselves arise.*"

He leaned forward slightly.

"Science explains mechanisms. Philosophy examines meaning. Ethics asks how to live. These are not rival domains—they are different scales of the same process. Like cells, organs, and consciousness. None can replace the others. None can be reduced to the others. Yet all are inseparable."

He lifted his hand, fingers loosely curved.

"Think of a river system. You can study the chemistry of water—that is science. You can reflect on what a river symbolises—that is philosophy. You can decide how to protect it—that is ethics. But the river itself flows regardless of which language you use. The mistake is not using one lens. The mistake is believing any single lens *is* the river."

Silence deepened.

"A non-reductive cosmology," Guruji said, "does not demand a single explanation for everything. It offers a *grammar*—a way to translate across scales without erasing difference."

He smiled faintly.

"Emergent coherence does not reduce mind to matter, nor dissolve matter into mysticism. It says: when relationships organise themselves with enough depth, something new becomes real—not imaginary, not supernatural, but *irreducible*."

Akanksh listened intently, his brow softening.

"So does this unify knowledge?" Guruji asked aloud, answering the deeper layer of the question. "Only if we abandon the desire for total control."

The lamps flickered once, then steadied.

"A true grand narrative does not explain everything," he said. "It teaches us how to *stand* in not knowing—without fragmenting."

He let the words rest.

"Coherent emergentism is not a final map of reality. It is a compass. It does not eliminate complexity; it teaches us how to live *responsibly* within it."

The hall felt fuller now, not with certainty, but with permission—to think deeply without forcing closure, to seek unity without violence to difference.

Guruji said softly, "When a worldview unifies without domination, it stops being a theory. It becomes a way of seeing. And when seeing changes, action follows."

No one spoke.

They did not feel as though they had been given an answer. They felt as though they had been given a place to stand—wide enough to hold science, philosophy, ethics, and the quiet mystery breathing beneath them all.

Outside, the night continued its patient unfolding.

Inside, something equally vast had found its shape—not as a grand conclusion, but as a living, listening coherence.

Akshatha sat quietly for a long while before speaking. Her eyes had the look of someone gazing through something—beyond words, beyond certainty. When she finally lifted her palms and asked her question, her voice was gentle, but it carried the tension of an honest struggle.

"Guruji," she said, "each discipline sharpens its own lens. Physics, biology, psychology, philosophy—each sees more clearly in its own way. And yet the sky remains fragmented. Can coherent emergentism truly unify knowledge without erasing difference? And if so… what would such unity demand of us, intellectually?"

The question lingered like incense smoke, slow to settle.

Guruji closed his eyes for a moment—not to retreat inward, but to let the room arrive fully. When he opened them, there was warmth there, but also precision.

"You have named the condition of modern knowing," he said softly. "A world of powerful telescopes—and a broken sky."

A few heads bowed, not in agreement, but in recognition.

"Each discipline," Guruji continued, "has learned to polish its lens until it can see astonishing detail. Physics sees the trembling of particles. Biology sees the choreography of cells. Psychology sees the patterns of the mind. Ethics sees the consequences of action. None of these is wrong."

He paused.

"The fracture does not come from difference," he said. "It comes from *forgetting that lenses are not the sky.*"

A subtle stillness moved through the hall.

"When a physicist says, 'Only matter is real,' or when a philosopher says, 'Only meaning matters,' or when an ethicist says, 'Only values guide us,' something essential is lost. Not because they are false—but because they are *partial.*"

He leaned forward slightly.

"Coherent emergentism does not ask disciplines to blur their focus. It asks them to remember their *place*."

Guruji lifted his hand, as though holding an invisible instrument.

"Imagine a telescope designed to see stars, insisting it can also measure the warmth of a hearth. Or a microscope demanding that galaxies come into focus beneath its lens. Knowledge breaks not because tools are sharp—but because they are misapplied."

A faint smile touched his face.

"Unity," he said, "is not sameness. Unity is *coordination*."

The word seemed to settle gently into the room.

"A symphony does not erase the violin by including the drum. It demands discipline, timing, and listening. Each instrument must know both its strength and its limit."

Akshatha's gaze softened.

"So what does such unity demand?" Guruji asked, answering her question as if completing a circle.

"It demands intellectual humility," he said. "The courage to say, 'This explains something—but not everything.'"

He continued, "It demands translation rather than conquest. To ask not, 'How can my discipline replace the others?' but 'How does my insight *interface* with them?'"

Silence deepened, not heavy, but attentive.

"And it demands patience," he added. "Because emergent coherence cannot be forced. It grows where boundaries are respected, and bridges are carefully built."

He looked around the hall, meeting faces one by one.

"Coherent emergentism is not a master theory sitting above all others," Guruji said. "It is a *relational stance.* A commitment to seeing how truths at one scale give rise to realities at another—without collapsing either."

Outside, a night bird called once, then fell silent.

"The sky appears fragmented," Guruji said, "not because it is broken—but because we are looking through instruments that were never meant to see it whole. The task is not to smash the lenses. The task is to learn how to *step back* far enough for the constellations to appear."

Akshatha lowered her eyes, something within her easing.

The hall remained quiet.

No one felt that the sky had been reassembled.

But something equally important had happened.

They had remembered that the sky was never truly broken—only waiting for a way of seeing patient enough, humble enough, and coherent enough to let its patterns emerge.

In the Buddha Hall, time no longer felt linear. It moved like breath—expanding, pausing, returning. The lamps flickered gently, casting halos of gold upon the quiet faces of the devotees. Outside, the moon had climbed higher, its light filtering through the latticed windows, laying pale paths across the stone floor as if inviting the mind to walk somewhere deeper.

Apeksha sat with her hands folded, her posture composed yet inwardly alert. There was a tenderness in her eyes—the kind that appears when intellect has reached its edge and is beginning to listen for something subtler. When she spoke, her voice was soft, but the question it carried was vast.

"Guruji," she asked, "does this framework truly *resolve* the hard problems—consciousness, meaning? Or does it simply *reframe* them as inevitable features of emergent layers?"

The room held its breath.

Guruji did not answer immediately. He looked at the moonlight on the floor, then at the lamps, then at Apeksha—as though tracing a continuity invisible to words.

At last, he spoke.

"We call it an explanatory gap," he said, "because we expect explanation to behave like a ladder—each rung taking us higher until we can finally look down and see the whole."

A faint smile crossed his face.

"But emergence," he continued, "is not a ladder. It is a *landscape*."

A few devotees shifted, leaning inward.

"When water becomes ice," Guruji said, "the molecules do not acquire a new substance. And yet hardness appears—something not found in the liquid. No physicist calls this a 'failure of explanation.' We accept that solidity is a property that *emerges* when conditions align."

He paused.

"But when awareness appears—when experience lights itself from within—we suddenly accuse reality of cheating."

A gentle murmur of understanding moved through the hall.

"The so-called hard problem," Guruji said, "arises from a hidden assumption: that explanations must reduce phenomena downward to simpler parts. Consciousness resists this not because it is mystical, but because it belongs to a *different level of organisation.*"

He turned his gaze back to Apeksha.

"Meaning and awareness are not missing pieces," he said. "They are *structural features* of certain emergent configurations—just as liquidity is a feature of water and melody is a feature of sound arranged in time."

The hall seemed to soften around the idea.

"Imagine," Guruji continued, "standing inside a cathedral and asking where the silence comes from. You can describe the stones, the arches, the physics of sound—but the *felt stillness* emerges only when space, form, and attention align. Would you say the silence is unreal because it cannot be weighed?"

Apeksha's breath slowed.

"Coherent emergentism does not dissolve the mystery," Guruji said gently. "It *relocates* it."

He leaned back slightly.

"Consciousness is not a ghost hiding in matter, nor a puzzle waiting for a final equation. It is what experience looks like *from the inside* when complexity crosses a certain threshold."

Outside, a breeze stirred the leaves, as though the world itself were listening.

"So does the framework resolve the hard problems?" Guruji asked, then answered himself. "No—if by resolve you mean eliminate. But yes—if by resolve you mean restore them to their rightful place."

He let the words settle.

"Meaning, too, is not an error in the system. It is not something we project onto a meaningless world. Meaning is what coherence feels like when it becomes self-aware."

Apeksha lowered her eyes, emotion welling—not confusion, but relief.

"The explanatory gap," Guruji said, "was never a chasm in reality. It was a fracture in our expectations. We were asking one layer of the world to speak the language of another."

The lamps flickered once, then steadied.

"In an emergent universe," he said softly, "not everything that is real can be reduced—and not everything that resists reduction is mysterious in the way we feared. Some things are simply *meant to be lived*, not dissolved."

The hall fell into a silence that was no longer searching.

It was listening.

And in that listening, consciousness did not need to explain itself.

It simply was.

Abhilasha sat near the centre aisle. Her face reflected a gentle tension—not resistance, but care. She was someone who loved clarity, yet respected mystery; someone who feared neither discipline nor depth. When she spoke, her voice carried that balance.

"Guruji," she asked, "does reframing the explanatory gap as *structural* rather than *temporary* deepen our understanding—or does it risk surrendering explanation too soon?"

The question fell into the hall like a stone into deep water—not loud, but far-reaching.

Guruji opened his eyes fully and looked at her for a long moment. There was no haste in him, no defensiveness. Only attention.

"You have named the real danger," he said quietly.

He rose from his asana and walked a few steps, stopping near a column where moonlight brushed the stone. He placed his palm against it, as if feeling the patience of centuries.

“Let me tell you a story,” he said.

“Once, two villages lay on opposite sides of a wide river. One village was known for its builders, the other for its philosophers. For generations, they argued about how to cross. The builders wanted measurements, materials, and timelines. The philosophers asked what it *meant* to cross—whether the crossing changed the traveller.”

A faint smile passed through the hall.

“One day, they began building a bridge together. But the river was vast, the currents strong. They reached the middle—and could go no further. The bridge stood unfinished, reaching out from both shores, suspended over depth.”

Guruji turned back to Abhilasha.

“Some said, ‘This proves the bridge is impossible.’ Others said, ‘This proves the bridge is sacred and must not be completed.’ Both were mistaken.”

The devotees listened, unmoving.

“The unfinished bridge was not a failure,” Guruji said. “It was a *diagnosis*.”

He returned to his seat.

"When we call the explanatory gap structural," he continued, "we are not declaring defeat. We are acknowledging the architecture of reality."

He held his hands apart, as if holding two invisible worlds.

"One shore is objective description—neurons, fields, equations. The other is lived experience—colour, pain, love, meaning. Consciousness does not sit on either shore. It *arises in the crossing.*"

Abhilasha's eyes widened slightly.

"To say the gap is temporary," Guruji said, "is to assume that one shore will eventually swallow the other—that experience will be reduced entirely to mechanism. That assumption is not humility; it is impatience dressed as confidence."

A gentle stillness spread.

"But," he added, his voice firming, "to call the gap structural does not mean we stop building. It means we stop building with the wrong expectations."

He leaned forward.

"The danger you sense arises only when 'structural' becomes an excuse for laziness—when mystery is used to protect ignorance. True structural humility does the opposite. It *demands better questions*, sharper methods, and deeper integration across layers."

Outside, a night bird called once, then fell silent.

"Consider music," Guruji said. "We can explain pitch, vibration, and harmony. Yet the sorrow in a raga, the lift in a symphony—these are not errors in acoustics. They are emergent meanings that exist only when sound meets a listening consciousness."

He paused.

"Would you say we surrendered explanation because we cannot reduce grief to frequency?"

Abhilasha lowered her gaze, understanding dawning.

"The unfinished bridge," Guruji said softly, "teaches us where explanation must transform, not retreat. It tells us that some truths are accessible only through *participation*, not conquest."

He looked around the hall.

"When science admits the gap is structural, it does not abandon rigour. It abandons arrogance. When philosophy admits it, it does not dissolve into vagueness. It becomes accountable to lived reality."

His voice softened.

"Consciousness remains partially unreachable not because it is forbidden, but because it is the *very medium through which reaching occurs.* The eye cannot see itself directly, yet it is not blind."

A long silence followed—rich, reflective.

"So no," Guruji said, meeting Abhilasha's eyes, "this reframing is not surrender. It is restraint. It is the wisdom to know when to push forward—and when to change how we walk."

The lamps flickered, then steadied again.

"The bridge is unfinished," he said, "not because the journey is over—but because crossing was never meant to end."

Abhilasha exhaled slowly. Something in her shoulders relaxed—not the relief of having an answer, but the peace of knowing that inquiry itself had been honoured.

In the Buddha Hall, the silence returned—not as a void, but as a living span between shores, quietly bearing the weight of all who dared to cross.

The previous silence had not ended; it had *opened.*

Akshaya, seated slightly to the left of the central aisle, had been listening with an intensity that was almost physical. His brow carried the mark of someone who had travelled through many books, many arguments, many frameworks—and had felt, more than once, the exhaustion of carrying them separately. When he spoke, his voice carried both urgency and care.

"Guruji," he asked, "how might embracing emergentism help us confront the modern epistemic crisis—disciplinary silos, relativism, even nihilism? Is this drive toward coherence merely a preference… or is coherence-seeking itself a cognitive imperative?"

The question did not fracture the silence. It *completed* it.

Guruji's gaze softened, not because the question was gentle, but because it was honest. He nodded once, slowly, as if acknowledging a familiar ache.

"You are naming the illness of our age," he said. "Not ignorance—but *disconnection*."

He gestured gently around the hall.

"Look at this space," he continued. "Stone, lamp, breath, listening—none of these explain the hall alone. Yet together, coherence arises. Remove the relationships, and all you have left are fragments. Modern knowledge has done something similar."

He paused, letting the analogy settle.

"We have trained our sciences to speak different languages, our philosophies to guard their borders, and our ethics to apologise for their own existence. Each discipline has become excellent—and lonely."

A faint murmur of recognition passed through the devotees.

"Disciplinary silos," Guruji said, "are not merely institutional failures. They are epistemic habits. We learn to ask questions that fit our tools, and then we mistake the limits of those tools for the limits of reality."

He leaned forward slightly.

"Emergentism offers a different posture. It does not ask, 'Which discipline is correct?' It asks, 'At what *level* does this truth arise?'"

Akshaya's eyes sharpened.

"Consider a city," Guruji said. "An economist studies flows of capital. A sociologist studies norms. An engineer studies infrastructure. A poet feels the city's soul at dusk. None are wrong. None are sufficient. The city *emerges* only when these layers are allowed to coexist without reducing one another."

He lifted his hand, palm upward.

"Fragmentation breeds relativism because, when truths cannot speak to one another, we assume none of them are grounded. And from relativism, nihilism follows—because meaning, once isolated, feels arbitrary."

The hall grew very still.

"But coherence-seeking," Guruji continued, "is not an ideology imposed from above. It is a *biological, cognitive, and existential instinct.*"

He touched his chest lightly.

"Your nervous system seeks coherence. Your emotions seek coherence. Your sense of self is not a fact—it is an emergent narrative that must hold together across time. When coherence collapses, we call it anxiety, depression, despair."

Akshaya swallowed softly.

"This is why nihilism hurts," Guruji said. "It is not merely a philosophical position. It is a symptom of prolonged incoherence."

He sat back.

"Emergentism counters this not by forcing unity, but by legitimising plurality within structure. It says: many truths, many methods—but not many *realities.* One reality, unfolding across scales."

Outside, the wind moved through the trees, sounding briefly like distant rain.

"So yes," Guruji said, answering Akshaya directly now, "coherence-seeking is a cognitive imperative—but not a tyrannical one. It is the same imperative that drives children to ask 'why,' that drives scientists to search for patterns, that drives lovers to make sense of one another's silences."

A gentle warmth entered his voice.

"When knowledge fragments, we suffer. When coherence grows, meaning returns—not as certainty, but as *orientation*."

He looked across the hall, meeting many eyes.

"Emergentism does not promise a final map. It offers a compass."

He turned back to Akshaya.

"And in a world drowning in information but starving for meaning," Guruji said softly, "the ability to seek coherence without erasing difference may be the most ethical intelligence we can cultivate."

Silence returned, but it was no longer heavy. It was aligned.

Akshaya lowered his head slightly, not in agreement alone, but in relief—like someone who had realised that the scattered pieces he carried were never meant to be held apart.

Inside, the air felt weighted—not with heaviness, but with consequence.

Padma her spine straight, her gaze steady yet searching. She had listened through the evening, through discussions of coherence and fragmentation, emergence and meaning. Yet something in her stirred uneasily—not a disagreement, but a recognition. When she spoke, her voice carried the calm gravity of someone asking not for theory, but for survival.

"Guruji," she asked, "is coherence-seeking truly a cognitive imperative? And what happens when societies lose the ability to integrate meaning across domains—when knowledge grows, but understanding does not?"

The hall seemed to inhale as one.

Guruji did not answer immediately. He looked upward, toward the dark wooden beams above, as though seeing something beyond them. When he finally spoke, his voice carried the texture of lived insight.

"Imagine," he said gently, "a tower built higher and higher, each floor stacked with exquisite precision. On one level—mathematics. On another—technology. On another—economics, psychology, art. The builders are brilliant. The materials are flawless."

He paused.

"But in their devotion to height," he continued, "they forget the stairs."

A subtle stillness moved through the hall.

"Knowledge accumulates," Guruji said, "but connection dissolves. Each floor becomes a world unto itself. Those who live on one level cannot visit the others—not because they are forbidden, but because there is no path."

Padma's eyes softened, as though she had recognised the structure.

"This," Guruji went on, "is what happens when coherence-seeking is dismissed as optional—when integration is treated as decoration rather than necessity."

He leaned forward slightly.

"Coherence is not a luxury of philosophers. It is how the mind survives complexity. The brain itself is an integration engine. It binds sight, sound, memory, and emotion into a single experience. When this binding fails, we do not call it pluralism—we call it *disorder*."

The word settled quietly, without accusation.

"At the societal level," Guruji said, "the same principle holds. When science advances without ethics, power grows without wisdom. When economics severs itself from ecology, prosperity eats its own ground. When technology outpaces meaning, speed replaces direction."

Outside, a night bird called once, then fell silent.

"What happens then?" Guruji asked aloud, answering Padma's question as much as the hall's unspoken fear. "Societies become efficient—and hollow. Informed—and confused. Capable of building everything except a future they can live inside."

Padma lowered her gaze, her hands tightening briefly in her lap.

"This is when people begin to feel unmoored," Guruji continued. "They sense that nothing fits together, so they retreat into extremes. Some cling to rigid ideologies that promise false unity. Others dissolve into nihilism, concluding that meaning itself is an illusion."

He shook his head slowly.

"But meaning was never lost," he said. "Only the *bridges* were."

He let the silence stretch, then softened his tone.

"Coherence-seeking is a cognitive imperative because reality itself is layered, relational, and nested. To refuse integration is not humility—it is amputation."

A faint intake of breath rippled through the listeners.

"Emergent coherence does not demand sameness," Guruji said. "It demands *conversation.* Between disciplines. Between generations. Between facts and values. Between what we can measure and what we must care for."

He looked directly at Padma now.

"When societies lose this ability, knowledge becomes a tower without stairs. Impressive from afar. Unlivable from within."

Padma's eyes glistened, not with sadness alone, but with clarity.

"So the work," Guruji said softly, "is not to slow knowledge—but to restore pathways. To teach not only how to know more, but how to *hold together* what we know."

The lamps flickered gently, as if in quiet agreement.

In the Buddha Hall, no one moved. Each devotee sat as though feeling the invisible stairways within themselves—fragile, necessary, waiting to be rebuilt.

And outside, beneath the moon's patient gaze, the world remained whole—still offering coherence to those willing to learn how to see it again.

Outside, the night had settled into maturity; even the insects seemed to hum with restraint, as if aware that something essential was being spoken.

Sam sat near the centre, his brow furrowed not with doubt, but with responsibility. He had followed the arc of the teachings—from emergence as explanation to emergence as ethic—but something pressed within him, asking to be grounded. When he spoke, his voice carried a practical urgency, almost tender in its insistence.

"Guruji," he asked, "if coherent emergentism is true—not just as an idea, but as the way reality actually works—what *concrete change* should follow? How must we live differently? Govern differently? Relate to non-human systems differently?"

The question landed like a stone dropped into deep water.

Guruji did not answer at once. He looked around the hall, meeting faces one by one—not to assess, but to include. When he finally spoke, his tone was gentle, but unmistakably firm.

"Truth," he said, "is never proven by elegance alone. It proves itself by what it *demands* of us."

He paused.

"If a truth changes nothing," Guruji continued, "it is either incomplete—or unreceived."

A quiet stirring moved through the hall.

"Imagine," he said, "a man who learns that the ground beneath his home is slowly eroding. If he merely admires the geological explanation but keeps building as before, we would not call him enlightened. We would call him *careless*."

A faint smile touched his lips, not unkindly.

"Coherent emergentism," Guruji said, "is such knowledge. It tells us that we do not live as isolated agents, but as nodes within living systems—social, ecological, technological, psychological—each influencing and being influenced."

He leaned forward slightly.

"If this is true, then the first change is not political or technological," he said. "It is *perceptual*."

Sam listened intently.

"We must stop asking only, 'What do I want?' or 'What works?'" Guruji said. "And begin asking, 'What patterns am I strengthening by my choices?'"

He let the question echo.

"In how we live," Guruji went on, "this means trading short-term optimisation for long-term coherence. Consuming less is not a sacrifice, but a respect for systemic balance. Speaking not merely to win, but to preserve relational trust. Measuring success not only by personal gain, but by whether the systems around us become more resilient—or more brittle."

The firelight reflected softly in the listeners' eyes.

"In governance," Guruji continued, "the change is profound. Leaders must stop behaving like engineers of outcomes and become gardeners of conditions. Policies must be judged not only by immediate results, but by the feedback loops they create—who gains voice, who is silenced, which behaviours are amplified, which futures are quietly foreclosed."

He raised his hand slightly, as if tracing an invisible web.

"A law that increases efficiency but erodes trust is not neutral," he said. "It is destabilising. A system that grows wealth while shrinking belonging is not successful—it is *fracturing.*"

Sam nodded slowly.

"And in our relationship with non-human systems," Guruji said, his voice softening, "the change may be the most humbling of all."

He gestured toward the open windows, where the night breathed gently into the hall.

"Forests, rivers, climates, even artificial intelligences—these are not merely tools or backdrops. They are emergent processes with internal coherence. To harm them is not simply to misuse resources; it is to destabilise the larger patterns that make our own lives possible."

A long silence followed.

"Coherent emergentism does not ask us to worship systems," Guruji said. "It asks us to *listen* to them. To act as participants rather than masters."

He looked directly at Sam now.

"The ultimate test," Guruji said, "is this:

Do our actions increase the capacity of the systems we touch to adapt, regenerate, and include—or do they narrow possibilities until collapse becomes inevitable?"

Sam felt something settle within him—not an answer to memorise, but a direction to walk.

Guruji closed his eyes briefly.

"When truth is lived," he said softly, "it becomes ethics. When ethics are embodied, they become culture. And when culture changes, the future follows—not by force, but by coherence."

The lamps flickered once, then steadied.

John had been quiet all evening. He was not restless, only watchful—like someone standing before a mirror, uncertain whether it would reflect his face or reveal something deeper. When he finally spoke, his voice carried neither challenge nor reverence, but sincerity sharpened by responsibility.

"Guruji," he asked, "if coherent emergentism is true—not just as an idea to admire, but as a way reality actually unfolds—what must *change*? In governance, technology, education, and even daily conduct? How does coherence become lived rather than merely understood?"

The question did not ripple outward. It sank inward.

Guruji remained still for a long moment. His gaze rested not on John alone, but on the space between all who were present—as if the answer itself needed room to arrive.

Then he spoke.

"A worldview," Guruji said softly, "is not a window. It is a mirror."

He let the words settle.

"What you believe reality to be," he continued, "will eventually be reflected in how you build, how you teach, how you govern—and how you touch one another's lives. You cannot hold a fragmented worldview and live a coherent life. Nor can you truly see coherence and continue to live as though nothing is connected."

He looked toward the lamps.

"If coherent emergentism is true," Guruji said, "then governance must abandon the fantasy of control."

A few heads lifted.

"Today, governance often behaves like a puppeteer," he went on, "pulling isolated strings—economy here, security there, environment elsewhere—hoping the whole will somehow dance. But systems do not respond to force the way objects do. They respond to *conditions.*"

He raised his hand slowly, as if opening a fist.

"Living coherence in governance means designing feedback, not commands. Listening mechanisms, not merely enforcement. Policies must be treated as hypotheses—revised when they distort trust, corrected when they concentrate power, abandoned when they harden systems instead of helping them breathe."

His voice deepened.

"A coherent society is not one without conflict," Guruji said. "It is one where conflicts do not metastasise into collapse."

John felt the truth of it like a weight—not heavy, but grounding.

"In technology," Guruji continued, "the change is even more urgent."

He paused, allowing the unspoken presence of machines, algorithms, and networks to enter the hall.

"Technology today is built to optimise attention, speed, extraction," he said. "But if reality is emergent, then every optimisation is also a *bias*—amplifying certain patterns while starving others."

He leaned slightly forward.

"To live coherence through technology," Guruji said, "we must design not for domination, but for dialogue. Not for engagement alone, but for meaning. Not for scale at any cost, but for resilience across contexts."

The metaphor came gently.

"A tool," he said, "should behave like a riverbank—not forcing the water, but shaping its flow so it nourishes rather than floods."

A hush deepened.

“In education,” Guruji went on, “the change may be the most subtle—and the most transformative.”

He looked around at the devotees.

“Education today fills minds like warehouses,” he said. “Facts stacked upon facts, disciplines sealed off from one another. But coherence cannot be memorised. It must be *cultivated*.”

His eyes softened.

“To live emergent truth, education must teach pattern recognition, systems thinking, and ethical imagination. Students must learn not only how things work, but how they *interact*. Not only how to solve problems, but how problems arise from misaligned systems.”

He smiled faintly.

“A coherent education,” Guruji said, “does not produce specialists who cannot speak to one another. It produces integrators who know when precision is needed—and when humility is wiser.”

John felt a quiet ache of recognition.

“And in daily conduct,” Guruji said at last, his voice lowering, “the mirror becomes unavoidable.”

He paused longer here.

"If coherence is real," he said, "then every action is relational. Every word is a ripple. Every habit is a vote for the kind of world that will emerge."

He looked directly at John now.

"Living coherence means noticing where your convenience creates hidden costs. Where your silence reinforces harmful patterns. Where your certainty prevents learning."

The hall seemed to breathe with him.

"It means choosing responses that stabilise relationships rather than fracture them. It means caring for your body as an ecosystem, your family as a system, your community as a living field—not possessions, but processes."

Guruji's voice grew almost tender.

"When coherent emergentism is lived," he said, "ethics stops being a rulebook. It becomes a form of *attunement*."

He closed his eyes briefly.

"And here is the final truth," Guruji said quietly. "You will know whether you believe this worldview not by what you argue—but by what kind of life begins to grow around you."

Silence followed—complete, unhurried.

John did not feel answered in the way one feels relief. He felt *claimed*—by a responsibility that could not be outsourced to theories or institutions.

And somewhere deep within the Buddha Hall, a mirror had been lifted—not to judge, but to reflect the life that was now being asked to change.

Guruji had been silent for a long while. His gaze rested gently on the floor before him, as if reading something written not in words but in patterns—of breath, posture, presence. When he finally spoke, it felt less like a conclusion and more like a careful placing of a final stone in an arch that had been rising all day.

Guruji said softly, "does not end with an answer. It ends with a position."

He lifted his eyes, meeting the circle not as teacher to students, but as one participant addressing others.

"You are not outside the world you seek to understand," he continued. "You are not standing at a distance, measuring emergence as though it were a river you observe from the bank. You are in the water."

A quiet stillness deepened.

"To live as a coherent node," Guruji said, "is to recognise that you are neither the master of the system nor a helpless fragment within it. You are a *participant*—a living junction where many streams meet."

He paused, letting the image take shape.

"Your body is a city of cells," he said. "Your mind is an ecosystem of thoughts, memories, instincts, and meanings. Your life is braided into families, markets, cultures, technologies, and climates. None of these were designed by you. Yet all of them respond—subtly, constantly—to how you move within them."

His voice carried warmth now, not instruction.

"A node does not control the network," Guruji said. "But it is not insignificant. Its health affects flow. Its distortions propagate. Its coherence stabilises paths that others may never see, yet still walk upon."

He gestured lightly toward the lamps.

"A single flame does not command the darkness," he said. "But it changes how the darkness behaves nearby. It creates orientation. It offers reference."

The devotees listened, not as seekers of transcendence, but as beings gently re-situated within the world.

"To live as a coherent node," Guruji continued, "means tending alignment across scales. It means noticing when your inner turbulence amplifies outer disorder—and when your clarity becomes a quiet stabilising force."

He looked slowly around the hall.

"It is humility without erasure," he said. "Responsibility without grandiosity. Participation without illusion of control."

The words landed like a deep breath after a long ascent.

"You need not save the world," Guruji said. "But you must stop pretending you are not shaping it."

A few smiles flickered—not of amusement, but of recognition.

"When you speak with care," he said, "systems soften. When you design with restraint, futures remain open. When you listen deeply, coherence has a chance to reorganise itself through you."

His voice lowered further.

"This is not heroism," Guruji said. "It is *attunement*."

He closed his eyes briefly, as if sealing the thought.

"To live as a coherent node," he said, "is to walk knowing that every step participates in a pattern larger than you—and that the pattern is not fixed. It is listening too."

Silence followed—not empty, not final, but alive.

Guruji remained seated for a moment longer, his eyes resting nowhere in particular, as though listening to something that did not require sound. The hall was utterly still. Even the lamps seemed to burn more quietly, their flames steady, disciplined, reverent. Then, without haste and without ceremony, he rose from his asana.

The movement itself felt like a benediction.

He offered a slight bow—not to the devotees alone, but to the silence that had held them all through the day. And then he walked out of the Buddha Hall, his footsteps unhurried, dissolving gently into the night. With that simple departure, the retreat did not *end*; it settled—like silt sinking to the bottom of clear water, leaving the surface calm, reflective, complete.

One by one, the devotees rose and left the hall. No one spoke. Words felt unnecessary, even intrusive. The Buddha Hall slowly emptied of its human congregation, yet it did not feel vacant. Its aura lingered—warm, resonant, as if the teachings had soaked into the stone, the wood, the air itself. The space seemed to breathe on its own now, carrying the soft imprint of Guruji's presence like a fragrance that remains long after the flower is gone.

Outside, the night had fully arrived.

The sky stretched wide and clear, a deep indigo canvas scattered with bright stars. Thin clouds drifted playfully, allowing the stars to appear and disappear, as though the heavens themselves were playing hide-and-seek. A gentle wind moved through the courtyards, whispering through leaves and branches, setting them into quiet conversation. Frogs croaked their nocturnal hymns to unseen water, insects hummed in a steady, rhythmic chorus, and somewhere in the distance, night birds called to one another—long, echoing notes that seemed to travel beyond the trees, beyond time.

Even in silence, the world was speaking.

Drawn by the hunger of the body now—simple, honest, grounding—the devotees moved toward the food centre for their meal. There was laughter there, but it was softer than usual. Plates clinked gently. Conversations unfolded slowly, like hands stretching after long stillness. Nourishment was taken with gratitude, as though eating itself had become a continuation of the day's teachings: participation without excess, presence without distraction.

After the meal, something unspoken drew a few of them together.

Vidyarthi, Aastha, Akshaya, Kiran, Padma, Vasudeva, and Abhirami found themselves near the old fireplace.

Someone had already lit it. Flames rose eagerly, licking the cool night air, their orange glow casting dancing shadows across faces relaxed by food and friendship. The fire crackled softly, a living presence that required no explanation.

They sat close, hands extended toward warmth, hearts opening in response. Their conversation meandered naturally—never forced, never structured. They spoke of moments from the day that had unsettled them, of questions that still hovered unanswered, of sudden recognitions that had arrived quietly and refused to leave. Laughter surfaced too—at forgotten notebooks, at stiff legs during long sittings, at the gentle absurdity of taking oneself too seriously.

Soon, others arrived, as if summoned by the fire itself.

Bhavya, Aarna, Dev, Kiran, Sam, Alice, Sofia, and John joined the circle, their faces still carrying the glow of a brief evening stroll. Nita, Lalitha, Rohith, and Sujitha came next, bringing with them fresh stories and renewed warmth. Moments later, Akshatha, Apeksha, Abhilasha, Akanksh, and Roopa appeared, their expressions reflective, alive with unfinished thoughts. Behind them followed Kieron, Astyn, Espen, Greta, and Divyani—quiet, attentive, content simply to be present. Soon, Aurora, Ginevra, Emma, Giorgia, Greta, Martina, and Beatrice completed the circle, until the fire was surrounded not just by bodies, but by shared stillness.

The flames flared, as though pleased.

For a while, no one led. The fire spoke. The night listened.

Then Kiran's voice rose—calm, steady, carrying a gentle expectancy.

"Time for Apeksha's story…"

The murmurs softened instantly. Faces turned. Even the fire seemed to settle, its crackle becoming rhythmic, attentive. Apeksha inhaled deeply. For a brief moment, her eyes closed—not in preparation, but in remembrance.

She began.

"There was once," she said, "a village built beside a vast river. The people loved the river, but they never questioned it. They drank from it, washed in it, planted their fields along its banks. They believed the river existed *for* them."

A few heads nodded. The fire shifted.

"One year," Apeksha continued, "the elders decided to improve the river. They built walls to straighten its flow, gates to control its floods, and channels to make it more efficient. The river obeyed—for a while. Crops flourished. The village prospered."

She paused.

"But slowly, fish disappeared. The soil hardened. Floods, when they came, were no longer gentle—they were violent. The villagers argued about who was responsible. Some blamed the builders. Some blamed the elders. Some blamed the river itself."

Her voice softened.

"One child, watching the river one evening, asked a simple question: *'Did we ever ask the river what it needed?'*"

Silence deepened.

"The villagers realised then that the river had never been a tool. It was a living pattern—responding, adapting, remembering. They had not meant harm. But they had forgotten the relationship."

Apeksha looked around the circle.

"So they began again—not by commanding the river, but by listening. They removed some walls. They restored curves. They allowed space for overflow. The river never returned to what it was—but neither did the village. They learned to live *with* it, not above it."

She fell silent.

The fire popped softly, sending a brief spiral of sparks into the night.

No one spoke for a long moment. The story did not ask for interpretation. It had already found its place.

One by one, the devotees rose. Movements were gentle, mindful, as though even standing required respect. Good nights were exchanged quietly, with smiles that carried more than words. As they walked toward their chambers, the lessons of the day travelled with them—not as concepts, but as felt alignments.

Each soul, like the embers left glowing in the hearth, carried a quiet light—subtle, enduring, ready to illuminate another day.

And thus, the night in Kanchipuram became more than darkness. It became a sanctuary. A bridge between what had been learned and what was yet to be discovered. A reminder that even in stillness, life's teachings continue to unfold—patient, interconnected, and constant as the stars watching silently above.

EPILOGUE

The Quiet Work of Coherence

"A human being is not an observer standing outside the pattern of reality, but a living participant within it, where even a single shift in awareness subtly reshapes the whole."

– *Shree Shambav.*

Every book must end. Every system, too, reaches a boundary—not always in collapse, sometimes in completion.

The Architecture of Coherence has traced a long arc: from particles to patterns, from minds to societies, from fragile systems to ethical horizons. Yet if this final volume has taught anything, it is this: **coherence does not conclude; it continues**. What ends here is not an argument, but an invitation.

Throughout these pages, emergence has been approached not as a mystery to be conquered, nor as a miracle to be revered, but as a *condition of reality itself.* Order arises without architects. Meaning persists without guarantees. Intelligence appears where no single intelligence commands it. And failure, when it comes, is rarely chaos invading order—it is order carried beyond its viable domain.

In this final movement of the series, coherence has been placed under pressure: societies fragment even as they coordinate, institutions shape lives despite lacking bodies, technologies learn faster than wisdom matures, and ethical responsibility disperses across systems too vast for individual blame. These tensions are not anomalies. They are signals. They tell us that the world we inhabit is not broken—but **deeply interconnected**, and therefore deeply sensitive to how it is shaped.

The question, then, is no longer *whether* emergence governs reality.

The question is **how we choose to live inside it**.

If coherence is real, then domination is an illusion.

If systems learn, then humility is not optional.

If flourishing is nested, then prosperity purchased through erosion is merely a delayed collapse.

And if responsibility is distributed, then ethics must move beyond judgment toward cultivation.

This book does not ask the reader to believe in a grand theory. It asks something more demanding: **to notice relationships where we were trained to see objects; conditions where we were trained to demand outcomes; participation where we were taught to seek control**.

The future described in these pages is not predetermined. Emergent systems do not obey prophecy. They respond to feedback. Small interventions, placed wisely, can redirect vast trajectories. Gentle hands can guide without gripping. Care, when practised consistently, can outperform force.

In that sense, this work ends where it must—**not with answers, but with orientation**.

You are not outside the system you seek to understand. You are not merely an observer of coherence. You are a *node within it*—shaping and being shaped, influencing and influenced, responsible not for mastery, but for participation.

The architecture of coherence was never hidden. It was simply waiting to be lived.

And so the final work does not belong to these pages. It belongs to the choices that follow—quietly, relationally, and under pressure.

Life Coach and Philanthropist

Shree Shambav is the visionary founder of the Shree Shambav Ayur Rakshita Foundation (www.shambav-ayurrakshita.org). He founded this institution with a lofty goal: to recognise human identity across gender, ethnicity, and nationality. Through this organisation, he wants to assist all communities in realising their full potential and the intrinsic beauty of life.

Shree Shambav, a Life Coach, is dedicated to supporting people on their journeys of self-discovery and empowerment. He assists people in discovering who they are, determining what inspires and drives them, and overcoming limiting ideas. His approach clarifies what one wants in life, assisting people through goal-setting and a step-by-step process for achieving them. He empowers people to make deliberate and responsible decisions, allowing them to identify their blind spots and evolve as individuals via the use of numerous strategies and tools.

The foundation's bold, uncompromising, and compassionate ventures are always aimed at initiating the "Inner Transformation" process. They focus on spiritual growth, personal growth, and self-healing while emphasising that true progress lies in "Inclusive Growth and Co-existence." This philosophy drives all their initiatives, encouraging a holistic approach to development and well-being.

Under Shree Shambav's leadership, the foundation has launched several impactful movements:

Shree Shambav Green Movement: This mission is to create a healthy, green, and clean earth through responsible water conservation and greening initiatives. The movement strives to make the world a green paradise by encouraging sustainable living and environmental responsibility.

Shree Shambav Vidya Vedhika (Vizhuthugal): This project aims to help students and children by offering training, books, stationery, and uniforms. It aims to provide the next generation with the tools and resources they need to excel both academically and personally.

Shree Shambav and his foundation exemplify the spirit of compassion, transformation, and inclusive growth via their work, which has a profound impact on individuals and communities around the world. His work exemplifies the power of acknowledging and nourishing the human spirit, creating a world in which everyone can reach their full potential and appreciate the beauty of life.

TESTIMONIALS

Journey of Soul - Karma - "We die in our twenties and are buried at eighty." Remember that nothing can stop someone who refuses to be stopped. "Most people do not fail; they simply give up." Shree Shambav deserves full credit. It allowed me to sit and consider what I might miss out on in life. The author has delved into every aspect of our daily lives. How can a seemingly insignificant change in these seemingly insignificant details bring us such joy? The Soul of Journey teaches you the "art of living" as well as the "art of dying."

Twenty + One Series - The rich cultural heritage offered a host in twenty + one short stories with incredible imagination, morals and values prevalent at a given time, influencing how people respond to a crisis or any situation. The author has recreated images with universal values and morals. The plentiful of fascinating from faraway lands would leave the modern play and story writers a cringe. The book supports trust and immeasurable values instilling hope for the new generations.

Death - "Shree Shambav's 'Death - Light of Life and the Shadow of Death' is an extraordinary masterpiece that delves deep into the profound questions surrounding our existence and mortality. The book's opening statement, 'Nothing ever truly dies; it simply ceases to exist in one form before resuming it in another,' sets the stage for a thought-provoking exploration of death's multifaceted nature. Shambav's remarkable ability to navigate the philosophical complexities of death and our universal fear of it is both enlightening and comforting. This book is a testament to the power of understanding and acceptance."

Whispers of Eternity - "Reading 'Whispers of Eternity' by Shree Shambav was a transformative experience that left me captivated from beginning to end. Each section of this exquisite collection delves into the myriad facets of existence, offering poignant reflections on life, death, and everything in between. Shree Shambav's verses are a testament to the beauty of language and the power of expression, inviting readers to embark on a journey of self-discovery and spiritual awakening. Whether celebrating life's simple joys or grappling with the complexities of human emotion, this book is a timeless companion that speaks to the heart and soul of every reader."

Life Changing Journey Series - "Life Changing Journey Series II Inspirational Quotes" is a remarkable collection that illuminates the path to self-discovery and personal growth. With its inspiring quotes and insightful reflections, this book serves as a beacon of light in a world often shrouded in darkness. Each quote offers wisdom, guidance, and encouragement, reminding readers of their inner strength and resilience. A must-read for anyone seeking inspiration and enlightenment.

Learn To Love Yourself – "A Heartfelt Guide to Authentic Self-Love." "Learn to Love Yourself" invites readers on a transformative journey to embrace their true essence in a world often focused on external validation. Through ten insightful chapters, it gently reveals principles of genuine self-love, guiding readers to deepen their connection with themselves. Beyond surface positivity, it encourages the cultivation of resilient self-acceptance, from embracing one's unique qualities to setting empowering boundaries. With inspiring stories and practical wisdom, this book is a trusted companion on the path to inner peace, fulfilment, and joy, helping readers build lives that reflect their authentic selves.

The Power of Letting Go – This book has been a gift to my spiritual journey. Shree Shambav's insights into attachment, personal growth cycles, and forgiveness are enlightening. The concept of seven-year cycles resonated with me, helping me understand the natural phases of life. I feel more empowered to let go of what no longer serves me and step into a life of freedom and fulfilment. A truly beautiful read!

A Journey of Lasting Peace – "A Journey of Lasting Peace" feels like a trusted friend guiding you through the maze of self-discovery. The 18 transformative principles are both practical and deeply resonant, addressing everything from gratitude practices to the art of letting go. Each chapter is infused with warmth and wisdom, making it easy to apply the concepts to my life. I particularly appreciated the emphasis on physical health's connection to mental well-being; it served as a wake-up call for me to prioritise my health. This book is an invaluable resource for anyone serious about personal growth!

Astrology Unveiled Series – "Profound, Logical, and Inspiring". What stands out in Astrology Unveiled is the author's dedication to making Vedic astrology logical and approachable. Each concept flows naturally into the next, backed by examples and exercises. The insights into karma and life cycles add a philosophical depth rarely seen in astrology books. Perfect for anyone seeking spiritual growth alongside astrological knowledge!

The Entitlement Trap - "Thought-Provoking and Challenging" The book challenges readers to confront their own sense of entitlement, and that's not easy—but it's essential. The Entitlement Trap doesn't offer a one-size-fits-all approach. Instead, it's a thoughtful, layered examination of how entitlement can limit our growth. The chapter on "Defining Your Own Hill" was particularly impactful, as it pushed me to reconsider which challenges are truly worth pursuing. A thought-provoking read for those willing to do the inner work to create a life they can be proud of.

Whispers of a Dying Soul – "A Soul-Stirring Reflection on Life's Unspoken Truths" - *Whispers of a Dying Soul: Unspoken Regrets and Unlived Dreams"* is a deeply moving exploration of the unexpressed emotions and unfulfilled aspirations that shape our lives in ways we often don't realise. This book invites readers to confront the powerful, often hidden impact of regret while guiding them through a journey of introspection and healing. Each page opens a space to reflect on the choices that define us—from moments of unspoken love to neglected passions—offering a gentle reminder to live authentically and courageously.

Whispers of the Soul: A Journey Through Haiku - is a mesmerising collection that speaks directly to the heart. Each haiku is a delicate brushstroke capturing life's fleeting beauty and timeless wisdom, inviting readers into moments of deep reflection and peace. This book is a balm for the soul, guiding us to find meaning in stillness and connection in simplicity. The themes of nature, love, and mindfulness echo universal truths, resonating with quiet, powerful grace. It's a book to be savoured slowly, cherished deeply, and returned to often. Truly, a gift for anyone seeking calm and clarity in life's chaos.

Whispers of Silence - Unlocking Inner Power through Stillness by Shree Shambav is a rare gem that beckons readers to pause, reflect, and reconnect with their inner selves. In a world that never stops talking, this book offers a profound exploration of silence—not as a void but as a rich and transformative space.

From the first page, Shree Shambav's writing resonates deeply, blending scientific insights with spiritual wisdom in a way that feels both universal and deeply personal. The author's ability to bridge the tangible and the transcendent makes this book an invaluable guide for anyone navigating the chaos of modern life.

The Power of Words: Transforming Speech, Transforming Lives - "The Power of Words is a profound and enlightening guide that has transformed the way I approach communication. Shree Shambav masterfully uncovers the hidden influence of our words on relationships, self-perception, and overall well-being. This book doesn't just teach you how to speak; it inspires mindful communication that fosters connection and trust. The insights on replacing negative patterns like gossip and judgment with kindness and authenticity are truly life-changing. The practical strategies and engaging narratives make it an invaluable resource for personal and professional growth. A must-read for anyone striving to communicate with intention, clarity, and compassion. Highly recommended!"

The Art of Intentional Living: Minimalism for a Life of Purpose - "The Art of Intentional Living is a refreshing guide to finding clarity in a cluttered world. With practical wisdom and profound insights, it inspires you to simplify, prioritise, and live with purpose. A must-read for anyone seeking balance and fulfilment."

Awakening the Infinite: The Power of Consciousness in Transforming Life - "Awakening the Infinite is a transformative guide that expands the mind and nourishes the soul. With profound insights and practical wisdom, this book beautifully explores the power of consciousness, helping readers connect with their true purpose and inner potential. It is a journey of self-discovery, healing, and spiritual awakening, offering clarity and inspiration at every turn. A must-read for anyone looking to live with greater awareness, meaning, and authenticity."

Beyond the Veil: A Journey Through Life After Death:

"This book touched me in ways few others have—it's not just about death, but about life, meaning, and the vast unknown that connects them. Beyond the Veil offers a graceful blend of science and spirit, inviting us to explore the mystery with awe rather than fear. The stories, insights, and reflections linger in your heart long after the final page. A truly transformative read that brings light on the shadows of mortality. It reminded me that in embracing death, we truly learn how to live."

Bonds Beyond Blood:

"A profoundly moving story that reminds us, family is not defined by blood, but by love, sacrifice, and the courage to heal. Every chapter touched my soul with its emotional truth and timeless wisdom. Through joy, grief, and redemption, this book captures the raw beauty of human connection. I saw reflections of my own family in its pages—both the pain and the hope. A powerful, unforgettable read that lingers long after the final word."

A Journey into Spiritual Maturity: 12 Golden Rules for Inner Transformation

"This book is a gentle yet powerful guide that awakened a deeper sense of purpose within me. Each golden rule felt like a mirror reflecting truths I needed to embrace. Shree Shambav's wisdom is timeless, poetic, and profoundly grounding. It's not just a read—it's a journey into the heart of who you truly are. A must-read for anyone seeking lasting peace, clarity, and inner transformation."

The Inner Battlefield: Overcoming the Enemies of the Mind and Soul:

"This book is a powerful revelation—an honest mirror to the battles we fight within. Every chapter is a step closer to clarity, peace, and emotional mastery. Shree Shambav brilliantly transforms ancient wisdom into practical guidance for modern souls. It awakened in me a new strength to face my fears and rise above inner turmoil. A must-read for anyone seeking true inner victory and lasting transformation."

The Seeker's Gold – Unlocking Life's Greatest Treasure

The Seeker's Gold is a soul-stirring masterpiece that goes far beyond the pursuit of wealth—it is a journey into the heart of what truly matters. Each chapter unfolds with poetic wisdom and emotional depth, revealing that life's real treasure is not found in riches but in the transformation of the self. As the protagonist evolves through trials, love, and profound realisations, so does the reader. This book is a mirror for every dreamer, a lantern for every seeker, and a companion for anyone walking the path of purpose. A timeless tale that stays with you long after the final page.

Born to Rise Series I & II:

Born to Rise – Series I & II is a profound awakening—a journey that begins in silence and leads you to the core of your true power.

Series I reshapes your understanding of success, showing that clarity is more valuable than applause, and authenticity more powerful than performance.

Series II takes you deeper, unlocking the mindset and inner strategy behind meaningful, lasting growth—not just in wealth, but in wisdom.

Together, these books are not just guides—they are soul mirrors, revealing the truths you've forgotten and the strength you've always held.

This is more than reading—it's remembering who you are, and rising with purpose, not pressure.

The Law of Attraction: A Soulful Path

The Law of Attraction: A Soulful Path is more than a guide—it's a spiritual companion. Shree Shambav has beautifully woven timeless wisdom with practical tools, helping me understand that manifestation isn't about control—it's about inner alignment and grace. Each rule in this book felt like a key unlocking something dormant within me. I've read many books on the Law of Attraction, but none touched my heart like this one. Through soulful rituals, deep reflection, and gentle encouragement, I began releasing old fears and stepping into clarity and peace. This book helped me move from desperation to trust, from wanting to becoming. It's a must-read for anyone yearning for meaning, healing, and true, lasting transformation.

Whispers of Stillness: Where the soul listens beyond the noise Series

Whispers of Stillness is a rare and luminous work that speaks softly yet transforms deeply. Each couplet feels like a breath of wisdom—gentle, precise, and profoundly awakening. Moving gracefully through Virtue, Wealth, and Love, the series invites quiet reflection, ethical clarity, and emotional truth. This is not poetry to rush through, but to live with. A timeless companion for seekers, leaders, and sensitive hearts, it restores stillness where the soul can truly listen.

ACKNOWLEDGEMENTS

To my grandfathers, grandmothers, mothers, fathers, aunts, uncles, neighbours, sisters, brothers, friends, and teachers, they poured in endless moral stories, retellings of Ramayana, Mahabharata, Puranas, Upanishads, and so on.

My teachers, neighbours, and kindred souls. Who provided us with a stage to perform wonderful Puranic stories and were gracious enough to acknowledge our efforts.

The artists and translators of epics have served as a source of inspiration, invigorating our spirits, making these works accessible, and enabling us to grasp the profound depths and deeper dimensions they contain.

I also cherish the stimulating conversations; I had with my wonderful mothers, Punitha Muniswamy and Uma Devi.

Our family's youngest member, Aadhya, who always overwhelmed me with questions, inspired this book.

I would likewise prefer to express gratitude to Mr Sivakumar, Mrs Roopa Sivakumar, Mr Akshaya

Rajesh, Ms Akshatha Rajesh, Ms Apeksha Prabhu, Mr Akanksh Prabhu, Mr Nikash Sarasambi, and Mrs Spoorthi Nikash for their valuable inputs.

I must thank Mr Rajesh, Mr Savan Prabhu, Mrs Revathi Rajesh, Mrs Rajani Sarasambi, and Mrs Manju Reshma, who encouraged me and often suggested writing a book. Their unwavering belief that I had something valuable to offer kept me going during my writing sessions.

Love you all,

Shree Shambav

Web: www.shambav.org

Email: shreeshambav@gmail.com

9 789357 808804

Printed at Repro India Ltd.